BANGLADESH
in Pictures

Tom Streissguth

Twenty-First Century Books

Contents

Website address: www.lernerbooks.com

Twenty-First Century Books
A division of Lerner Publishing Group, Inc.
241 First Avenue North
Minneapolis, MN 55401 U.S.A.

web enhanced @ www.vgsbooks.com

Library of Congress Cataloging-in-Publication Data

Streissguth, Thomas, 1958–
      Bangladesh / by Tom Streissguth.
         p.   cm. – (Visual geography series)
      Includes bibliographical references and index.
      ISBN 978-0-8225-8577-0 (lib. bdg. : alk. paper)
      1. Bangladesh—Juvenile literature. I. Title.
   DS393.4.S78 2009
   954.92—dc22   2007044717

Manufactured in the United States of America
1 2 3 4 5 6 – BP – 14 13 12 11 10 09

INTRODUCTION

The short history of the independent People's Republic of Bangladesh is filled with struggles familiar to developing countries. Bangladesh is home to more than 150 million people, who live in a nation roughly the size of Iowa. The country has few natural resources other than fertile land. Industry is limited, and the political system is steeped in violence and corruption. A harsh climate and flat topography, or landscape, add to Bangladesh's challenges. The low-lying nation is vulnerable to flooding, and the high winds and heavy rainfall of the annual monsoon often devastate coastal areas.

At one time, the region around the lower Ganges River was known as Bengal. It was a thriving center of rice growing and textile making. Foreign explorers and merchants who came to Bengal found a fertile and productive land. In the eighteenth century, Great Britain established control of the region and the rest of northern India. The British sought to lessen competition among textile industries in their

Indian colony and in their distant home islands. As a result, Bengal developed few new industries. It became primarily a source for basic agricultural goods such as rice and jute (used to make twine and sacks for bulk goods such as grain and tobacco).

The result was very slow development of manufacturing in the region. As the population grew, the people of eastern Bengal struggled to survive on the land's limited resources. The migration of rural people into cities in the twentieth century brought a rising tide of poverty. Meanwhile, religious and economic rivalry between followers of the religions of Hinduism and Islam sparked violence. In 1947, when Great Britain granted independence to India, eastern Bengal became part of East Pakistan, a Muslim majority nation. A mass migration of people across the border of East Pakistan and India further disrupted Bengali society.

East Pakistan finally broke away from Pakistan in 1971, renaming itself Bangladesh. Fighting in the Indo-Pakistani War (1971) devastated

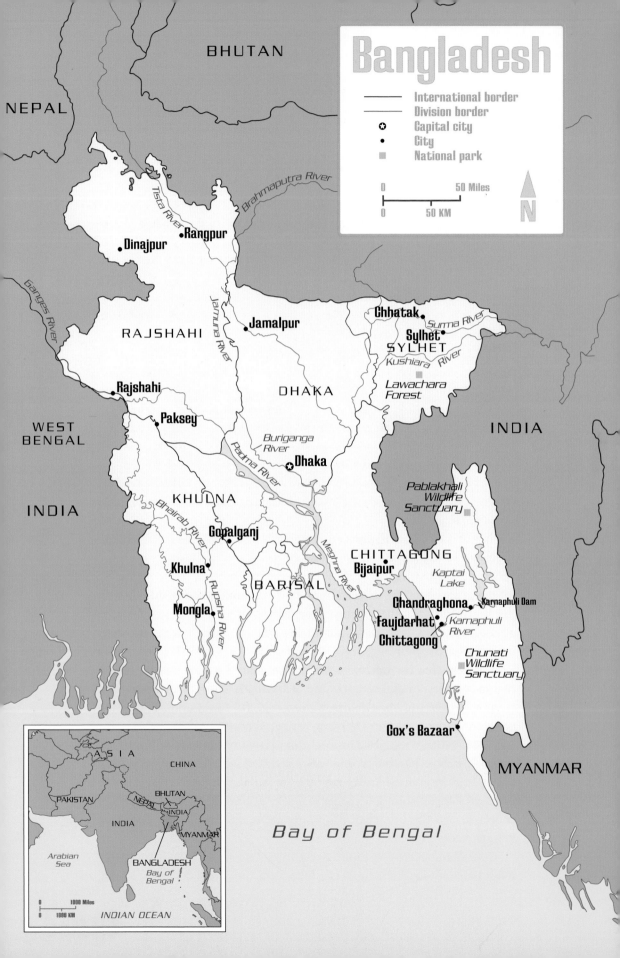

the capital of Bangladesh, Dhaka, and other cities as Indian army units crossed the border and battled the Pakistani army. The war left a damaged industrial base and an uneasy relationship between civilian and military sectors. The army of Bangladesh still plays a leading role in the government. Military leaders have taken control several times and in the twenty-first century still overshadow political life, elections, and the legislature.

Bangladesh takes pride in its rich Bengali culture, which it shares with the region of West Bengal in neighboring India. The people of Bangladesh hold to many ancient customs in marriage and family life. Music, art, dance, and literature draw on popular styles developed centuries ago. While Muslims (followers of Islam) make up a majority, the country remains tolerant of other faiths, including Hinduism, Buddhism, and Christianity.

In the twenty-first century, the economy of Bangladesh has undergone big changes. Bangladeshis work in a small but growing technology sector as well as a thriving garment business. Low factory wages have prompted violent protests, which brought some improvements in working conditions. A "microcredit" industry loans small amounts of money to poor families to set up small businesses. In addition, many Bangladeshis have moved abroad in search of better-paid work, including construction projects in the Middle East. Many of these workers send a part of their wages home, improving economic conditions for families as well as the entire nation. In the future, visitors drawn by the country's historical sites and fascinating culture may contribute to a new and productive tourist industry.

Bangladesh struggles with a weak overall economy, frequent natural disasters, harmful effects of global warming, overcrowding, poor health conditions, and a political system in frequent turmoil. Rivalry among the leading political parties results in street fighting, military action, and dictatorship (rule by leaders with total authority). Many people have fled the nation, while those who remain deal with a lack of opportunity and a low standard of living. A European Union committee on climate change announced in 2008 that Bangladesh, with so much of its land barely above sea level, could be one of the countries hardest hit by global warming and rising ocean levels. These and other complex problems illustrate the challenges that Bangladesh, along with many other young countries, face in overcoming a difficult history.

THE LAND

Bangladesh is a small and low-lying nation of south Asia. It is at the northern limits of the Bay of Bengal, an arm of the Indian Ocean. The country covers 55,598 square miles (144,000 square kilometers), making it about the same size as Iowa. India borders Bangladesh to the west, north, and east. Bangladesh and Myanmar (formerly Burma) share a boundary of 120 miles (193 km) in the southeast. At its widest point, Bangladesh is about 410 miles (660 km) from west to east. It is 509 miles (820 km) from north to south.

Topography

Bangladesh contains four major regions: the Bangladesh Plain, the Sylhet Hills, the Chittagong Hills, and the Mouths of the Ganges. A complex network of wide rivers and their smaller tributaries (branches) covers the Bangladesh Plain. This flatland makes up 80 percent of the country. The rivers are important for transportation, but flooding during the monsoon season is a constant threat. The rivers also provide

resources such as fresh fish, a staple of the Bangladeshi diet, and fertile soil, carried by the rivers from the highlands to the north.

The land rises in the Sylhet Hills, in the northeastern corner of Bangladesh near the border with India. A series of low ridges runs north and south in this region, which is part of the highlands that divide the Indian subcontinent and Southeast Asia. Flat basins between these hills often flood during the monsoon season, making transportation difficult. A series of small lakes fill the lowlands in the valley of the Surma River.

The Chittagong Hills in the southeast form a distinct highland region. Small streams there have cut narrow valleys through a lush tropical forest. The Chittagong Hills form the foothills of a mountainous region stretching from western Myanmar north to the Himalaya mountains (the world's highest mountain range). Mount Keokradong, at 3,196 feet (974 meters), rises near the meeting point of India, Myanmar, and Bangladesh. Long claimed as the highest point in Bangladesh, Keokradong's status is in question. Some geographers

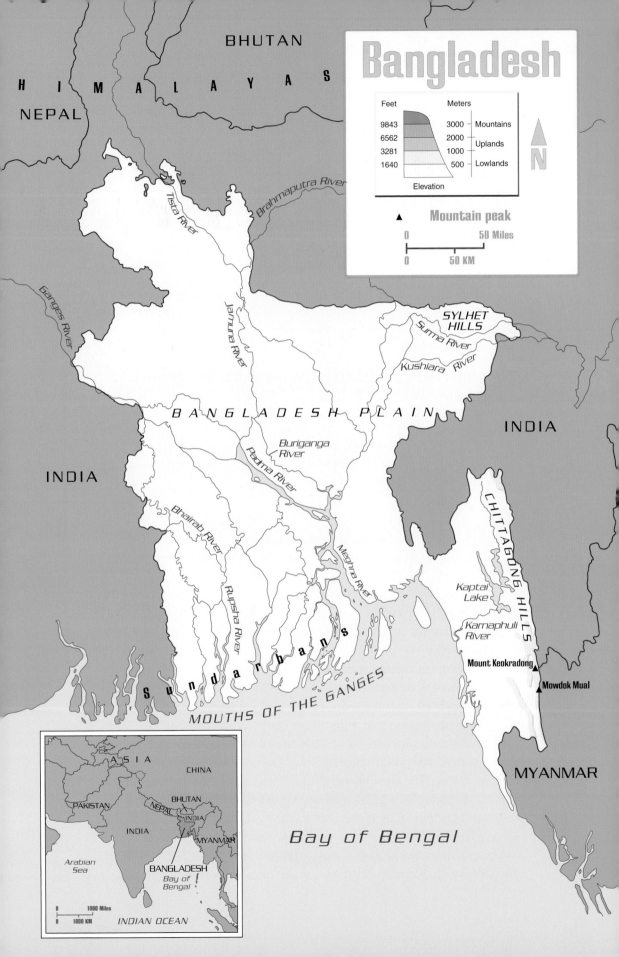

The Sundarbans lies in the **Mouths of the Ganges region** in Bangladesh. The Sundarbans is the largest mangrove forest in the world.

claim that an unnamed peak on the Myanmar-Bangladesh border rises to 3,451 feet (1,052 m).

An ever-changing river delta (the fan-shaped area of deposits at the mouth of a river) stretches along the southern coast of Bangladesh. Known as the Mouths of the Ganges, this region is lined by hundreds of streams flowing southward into the Bay of Bengal. The rivers run among sand dunes, small islands, and heavy tropical forest that blocks any form of transportation. A mangrove forest known as the Sundarbans grows where the sea meets the land. Mangroves are short trees and shrubs that thrive in flooded and marshy coastal areas. Bangladesh has protected much of the Sundarbans as a forest and wildlife preserve.

Rivers

An immense web of more than seven hundred rivers and thousands of smaller streams marks the landscape of Bangladesh. These rivers often flood during monsoon season. The heavy flooding can destroy or damage villages in low-lying areas. The rivers of Bangladesh also commonly change their courses. Because the land is flat, the waterways easily shift from one place to another, flooding new areas and leaving old courses dry. In the twentieth century, dams and canals channeled rivers to limit this natural shifting.

The main branch of the Ganges River flows into Bangladesh from the west. The Ganges begins in the foothills of the Himalayas. It flows eastward for 1,557 miles (2,510 km). Then it turns south to meet the Jamuna River west of Dhaka. It carries large amounts of rich silt (small bits of soil) downstream to its delta. The cities and industries that line its banks also heavily pollute the river.

The Jamuna originates in the north, at the confluence (meeting) of the Brahmaputra and Tista rivers. Each spring this waterway swells with snowmelt from the Himalayas and the highlands of Tibet, far to the north. The rough Jamuna constantly shifts its course, creating and destroying small mud islands and making permanent settlement along its banks impossible.

At the confluence of the Ganges and the Jamuna begins the Padma River, which receives the waters of more than one hundred tributary streams. The Padma flows 78 miles (126 km) to a meeting with the Meghna, a river that flows southward from the Sylhet Hills. The Meghna is the longest waterway in Bangladesh, running for 416 miles (670 km). In its lower reaches, the Meghna measures several miles across. The river divides into a delta of several large streams and empties into the Bay of Bengal.

A boat floats along on the **Meghna River** in southern Bangladesh. For links to websites with more information on this and other rivers in Bangladesh, visit www.vgsbooks.com.

A separate watershed (area drained by a river and its tributaries) lies in the Chittagong region, with its main stream the Karnaphuli River. This waterway originates at the Karnaphuli Dam. The dam, which generates most of the country's hydroelectric power, created the artificial Kaptai Lake. The Karnaphuli flows rapidly through the Chittagong Hills and empties into the Bay of Bengal at the city of Chittagong.

Bangladesh is attempting to control the flow of its rivers. Canals channel floodwaters, while berms (earthen dams) protect low-lying towns. Irrigation systems keep saline (salty) seawater from damaging crop fields. But the water table is falling in some parts of the country, as people are drawing more water from underground wells and aquifers. As a result, some rural areas of Bangladesh don't have enough water for crops and for household use during the dry season.

◉ Climate

The climate of Bangladesh varies between dry and rainy seasons. The growing cycle of Bangladeshi agriculture closely follows the seasons. Spring is a hot and humid period that allows planting and cultivation. Temperatures at this time of year rise to 100°F (38°C).

A late-spring monsoon begins in

THE STORM THAT STARTED A COUNTRY

One of the deadliest storms in history struck East Pakistan on November 12, 1970. The cyclone (a storm similar to a hurricane) caused a high surge of water that flooded thousands of villages and drowned half a million people. The Bhola Cyclone had effects far beyond the flooding and loss of life. The government of Pakistan was slow to respond with emergency medical help. With no food or freshwater, many people suffered and died. The poor response prompted a civil war the following year. With India's help, East Pakistan won its independence and became Bangladesh.

Villagers search for rice and other grains to salvage after the Bhola Cyclone in 1970.

June, caused by a rush of cooler air from the sea that meets hot air lying over the Bangladesh Plain. Heavy thunderstorms swell the rivers, while the strong southerly winds push tidal waters inland. The result can be disastrous floods that wash away crops and destroy roads and bridges. Monsoons also cause heavy damage, disease outbreaks, and starvation in isolated towns and villages.

The rains continue through October—the harvest season—when a cooler and drier season dries out the land. Winter continues through January, the coolest month of the year, when temperatures average about 50°F (10°C). In March, spring arrives and temperatures and humidity begin to rise again.

The heaviest rainfall occurs in the northeastern Sylhet area, with 200 inches (508 centimeters) or more falling every year. Rajshahi, a city on the western border, is the driest spot in Bangladesh. It receives about 55 inches (140 cm) per year. The capital, Dhaka, has an annual average temperature of 77°F (25°C). Most of its annual rainfall of 73 inches (185 cm) falls during the summer monsoon season.

Flora and Fauna

The fertile soil and heavy rain of Bangladesh nourish natural forests and thriving wetlands in more remote areas of the country. The Sundarbans is home to the largest mangrove forest in the world. Small mudflats and coastal islands lie among the mangroves, which are home to a wide variety of fauna. Mangroves protect the coastal areas from flooding and tidal surges. They also help prevent erosion (the wearing away of land) by slowing the large waves that come ashore during storms.

The hills of Chittagong and Sylhet support thick stands of bamboo. Tropical hardwoods such as teak and mahogany grow in the southeastern highlands. Ferns and hyacinth thrive in well-watered areas. The national flower is the water lily. It sports bright pink or white flowers and blooms in the hot spring months along the riverbanks.

Despite human overcrowding, Bangladesh boasts a large array of wildlife. The endangered Bengal tiger roams the

Water lily

Bengal tigers roam the Sundarbans in Bangladesh. This tiger lives at the zoo in Dhaka, the capital of Bangladesh.

Sundarbans, as does Bangladesh's national animal, the spotted deer. Black bears thrive in the Sylhet Hills of the northeast. Small populations of water buffalo, rhinoceros, and gibbons (small apes) have survived despite the encroaching towns and farms. Crocodiles, turtles, frogs, lizards, and snakes—including cobras—are also common. In the rivers and along the seacoast, crustaceans including shrimp, lobsters, and crabs abound. Blue whales are sometimes spotted near the shores of the Bay of Bengal.

Bangladesh lies along an important migratory route for birds. Some of these birds arrive in the winter months from distant Europe or Siberia, Russia. Ducks, geese, cranes, and other birds favor wetlands and rivers. Bangladesh has made the sweet-singing doel, or magpie robin, its national bird.

Natural Resources

Bangladesh benefits from the millions of tons of fertile silt that its rivers deposit each year in the spring and summer floods. The nutrient-rich soil moves downriver and overflows riverbanks. It spreads across fields where farmers grow rice, sugarcane, jute, and other crops.

FROGS COME HOME!

For many years, Bangladesh exported frog legs as a food product. As the number of frogs in the wild declined, insect populations rose. The insects—especially mosquitoes—that the frogs normally ate became a big problem by spreading deadly diseases such as malaria. Bangladesh began limiting frog exports in 1989 to keep the mosquito numbers in check.

Natural gas deposits exist in northeastern Bangladesh, as well as offshore in the Bay of Bengal. Small oil reserves are found near Chittagong and in the Sylhet Hills, as are deposits of iron ore and the mineral titanium. The nation has a few coal mines near the town of Jamalpur. But Bangladesh lacks the money and foreign investment to fully exploit this resource.

In the Sundarbans, a salt-making industry uses seawater that annually floods the coastal plains. Limestone deposits in the Sylhet region produce stone for construction and an important ingredient for cement. Bamboo forests in the east provide materials for making furniture and weaving mats. Kaolin (white clay) from the Bijaipur area of southern Bangladesh goes into the clay mixture that many households use to make pottery. Bangladesh also benefits from the abundant fish that swim its rivers and from offshore schools of fish and crustaceans.

Environmental Challenges

Bangladesh faces many environmental problems. The country is severely overcrowded. Some areas of Dhaka and other urban centers are home to an average of more than 20,600 people per square mile (8,000 per sq. km). Some of these urban areas lack proper drainage systems. This causes pollution of waterways and public water supplies. In addition, heavy traffic chokes the city centers, often creating thick clouds of smog. As the cities spread, development destroys natural habitats and hinders the natural drainage of the land.

The wildlife of Bangladesh is under pressure from spreading cities, the destruction of forests, and the cultivation of land. Several large mammal species, including the Bengal tiger, are endangered and are protected from poaching (illegal hunting). Still, because tigers, crocodiles, and other species pose a threat to people, many are killed or captured. The Chunati and Pablakhali wildlife sanctuaries in the Chittagong Hills, the Lawachara Forest in the Sylhet region, and three separate preserves in the Sundarbans provide a last refuge for many species.

As farmers cultivate more areas of the countryside, natural forests and wetlands disappear. This leads to soil erosion and further flooding. Monsoon floods carry salt water inland, a problem for farmers. Agricultural pesticides end up in waterways used for drinking water and for commercial fishing. The rivers that carry fertile soil to fields also bring waterborne diseases such as cholera. Poor sanitation serves to spread these diseases. Although many wells have been dug to provide clean water, many of these wells are polluted with arsenic, a poison that exists naturally in the soil.

These children live in a **fishing village** in southwestern Bangladesh. This thatched-roof hut is made out of mud.

Bangladesh is working to address these problems. Flood-control systems control watercourses. Pumps and drainage systems treat waste products before they reach the rivers. The government has set several areas aside as wildlife refuges.

One environmental threat Bangladesh can't control is global warming. A changing global climate threatens to disrupt the monsoon season, which could cause millions of people to lose crops, income, or even their lives. A rise in sea levels, caused by melting polar ice, also poses a serious threat to Bangladesh, since much of the nation's land lies only a few feet above sea level.

Cities

Cities, towns, and villages dot the landscape of Bangladesh. About 23 percent of the nation's population lives in urban areas. As its population continues to grow, this percentage will rise.

Visit www.vgsbooks.com for links to websites with additional information about the cities in Bangladesh.

Traffic can be seen clogging the streets of Dhaka in this view from above. Millions of people live in Dhaka, the largest city in Bangladesh.

DHAKA is the capital and the largest city of Bangladesh. It sprawls across a plain spreading from the eastern bank of the Buriganga River, in the center of the country. The population of the city is about 12 million, ranking it among the most populous in the world.

Dhaka began as a series of small towns. They eventually gathered into a larger metropolis that flourished at the time of the Mughal Empire in the eighteenth century. A rival of Kolkata (Calcutta) when the British ruled India, Dhaka became the capital of East Pakistan on the independence of Pakistan in 1947. During the Indo-Pakistani War of 1971, the city suffered heavy damage and loss of life. Dhaka emerged as the capital of independent Bangladesh in 1972.

Modern Dhaka is the political and cultural heart of Bangladesh, as well as the country's most important industrial center. Dhaka suffers from severe overcrowding, however. Its largest slum is home to more than 100,000 people. A high crime rate, pollution, a lack of clean water, and heavy traffic affect the quality of life. Yet the city still attracts a steady stream of migrants from the countryside, who arrive to seek jobs. Foreign investors have also arrived to build factories and invest in Bangladeshi businesses.

CHITTAGONG, the second-largest city of Bangladesh, is home to about 4 million people. It is a port city in the southeast, lying near the Karnaphuli

River and the coast of the Bay of Bengal. The city serves as an important transit point for goods moving into and out of the country.

Chittagong has been a thriving port since the sixth century. Its modern factories produce shoes, frozen seafood, steel, cars, and clothing. A shipbreaking industry employs workers at the nearby city of Faujdarhat. Workers break apart old ships in the difficult and often dangerous salvage of scrap metal, used oil, fixtures, tools, and other useful items.

KHULNA is the nation's third-largest city, with about 1.5 million people. Located on the Rupsha and Bhairab rivers in southwestern Bangladesh, the city connects to the sea through the port of Mongla, about 40 miles (64 km) to the south. Khulna is in the center of a thriving agricultural region where farmers grow rice, sugarcane, and tobacco. A jute-milling (processing) industry and small river shipyards are leading employers.

RAJSHAHI is the largest city of northern Bangladesh, with about 800,000 people. It lies on the Padma River and the western border with India. The city is famous for its thriving silk industry. It is also a market center for locally grown rice, lentils, sugarcane, and fruit. Rajshahi is home to several important Muslim shrines and mosques (Islamic houses of prayer). An express train known as the Silk City Express links Rajshahi with Dhaka.

Palm trees and buildings are seen in this aerial view of Chittagong.

HISTORY AND GOVERNMENT

Humans were living in the region known as Bengal (and later as Bangladesh) long before recorded history. Scientists have discovered stone tools in the region dating to several thousand years B.C. At some point, the people of Bangladesh developed metal tools or began trading for them.

Migrations brought people from northern Asia as well as settlers from Southeast Asia. Other groups, including the Tibeto-Burmans from the Himalayas to the north and Dravidians from southern India, also migrated to Bengal. A central Asian people known as the Aryans (or Indo-Aryans) arrived in northern India by 4000 B.C. The Aryan literature known as the Vedas gave rise to a belief system known as the Vedic culture (the root of modern Hinduism, the oldest continuing religion in the world). A Dravidian people known as the Bang also settled in the area about 1000 B.C.

In the Ganges River delta, several kingdoms including Pundranagara and Vangala arose. These realms absorbed many parts of Vedic and

Aryan society. They were strong enough to mount military expeditions to the island of Ceylon (modern Sri Lanka) and colonize parts of the major islands of the East Indies. Trade routes linked northern India with Southeast Asia and the Middle East. Merchants profited from trade in spices, cloth, precious gems, and other luxuries between eastern Asia and the Mediterranean region.

By the fourth century B.C., a kingdom known as Gangaridai held sway over the lower Ganges River and the Bengal region. Ancient Greek and Roman writers described Gangaridai as a powerful kingdom. According to one account, a royal palace and capital were built in the city of Gange, which archaeologists have yet to locate. Other historical sources claim that Gangaridai's massive army deterred Alexander the Great, a Macedonian (Greek) general, from continuing his invasion of India in the 330s B.C.

Alexander appointed local satraps (governors) to rule in his name as he marched west out of India. As Alexander withdrew, however, the

ALEXANDER THE GREAT THINKS TWICE

In the 320s B.C., Alexander the Great was leading a great army through India. But the fearsome kingdom of Gangaridai and its corps of war elephants turned Alexander back. In his book *Indica*, the ancient Greek traveler and historian Megasthenes tells the story:

"Now this river [the Ganges] . . . flows from north to south, and empties its waters into the ocean forming the eastern boundary of the Gangaridai, a nation which possesses a vast force of the largest-sized elephants. Owing to this, their country has never been conquered by any foreign king: for all other nations dread the overwhelming number and strength of these animals. . . . Alexander the Macedonian, after conquering all Asia, did not make war upon the Gangaridai, as he did on all others. For when he had arrived with all his troops at the river Ganges, and had subdued all the other Indians, he abandoned as hopeless an invasion of the Gangaridai when he learned that they possessed four thousand elephants well trained and equipped for war."

small states of northern India were thrown into turmoil. In the midst of conflict among the satraps, the ambitious king Chandragupta Maurya founded the Mauryan Empire in 322 B.C. The Mauryan realm extended from southern India to present-day Pakistan, Afghanistan, and Bangladesh. The most famous king of this realm, Asoka, ruled from 273 to 232 B.C. He helped spread the Buddhist faith (which had arisen in India about two hundred years earlier) throughout the Indian subcontinent and as far as the island of Sri Lanka.

The Gupta Empire

A series of weak kings followed Asoka. The Mauryan Empire began to decline. Brhadrata, the last king of the dynasty (family of rulers), was killed by his commander in chief, Pusyamitra Sunga, in 185 B.C. The kingdom of Sunga then emerged in northeastern India and Bengal, with its capital at Pataliputra (modern-day Patna, India). Pusyamitra Sunga persecuted Buddhists and returned his realm to the old Vedic traditions.

The Kanva dynasty overthrew the Sunga realm in the first century B.C. But it vanished after just a few generations. The much larger and more powerful Gupta dynasty replaced it in the third century A.D. The Gupta dynasty spread its authority across south Asia, from the plain of the Ganges River to present-day Nepal and Pakistan. The Gupta kings brought an era of peace and stability to Bengal. The sciences of astronomy and mathematics made important advances under the Gupta rulers. The kings also supported the arts. Many of the most important shrines and monuments of Bengal rose during this period.

Bengal became a crossroads linking Burma to the east, China to the north, and the plain of the Ganges River to the west. Under the Gupta dynasty, Bengal's coasts served as a center of trade. Merchant ships carried goods—as well as Buddhism—from the Indian subcontinent to Sri Lanka and Southeast Asia. In the fourth century A.D., the Gupta king Samudragupta conquered several nations to the south, turning their kings into vassals (rulers obliged to pay an annual tribute). He supported the worship of traditional Hindu gods and goddesses. But he also tolerated Buddhism within the Gupta domain.

An invasion of the Huna people of Afghanistan weakened the Gupta dynasty in the early sixth century. Meanwhile, a smaller realm known as Samatata, ruled by Buddhist kings, emerged in eastern Bengal. The capital of this realm, Devaparvata, held a flourishing royal court. At this time, the earliest form of the Bengali language emerged. This "proto-Bengali" became an important medium for poets and storytellers, who laid the foundations of modern Bengali literature.

After the Gupta dynasty fell in 550, a series of small and weak dynasties ruled Bengal. None of these realms could unify the region, however. Bengal saw frequent battles between competing princes. Geography played an important role in this history. The lower Ganges plain, with its maze of rivers and marshes, proved impossible for any one ruler to seize and govern. Buddhism, however, remained strong in Bengal through all of this turmoil. As the Hindu caste system (a social organization based on strict classes) grew strong in India, the people of eastern Bengal held to Buddhist beliefs. Others worshipped local gods and spirits.

The Buddhist king Gopala, elected by the princes of Bengal to his throne in 750, founded the Pala dynasty. The Pala kings controlled Bengal and much of eastern India. Scholars founded the first universities in Bengal. Buddhist missionaries (religious teachers who spread their faith) taught their beliefs in Nepal, Tibet, and Southeast Asia. The Pala kings exercised religious tolerance and ended many centuries of rivalry between Hindus and Buddhists. By the ninth century, the Pala kings ruled a vast territory across northern India, from Bengal to present-day Afghanistan. They established trading posts and colonies in Malaysia and the major islands of the East Indies.

In 1095 the prince Hemanta Sen seized power in Bengal. He was the first of a series of kings, known as the Sena rulers, who took the authority of the Pala kings in the region and established a new Hindu dynasty.

The Dhakeshwari Temple in Dhaka is the nation's most important temple.

The Sena rulers opposed Buddhist practice. They imposed the strict caste system of Hinduism in Bengal. They also raised the famous Dhakeshwari Temple in Dhaka. It remains the country's most important Hindu shrine.

The Islamic Conquest

In 1205 an army from central Asia, under the Turkish commander Bakhtiar Khilji, arrived in Bengal. Khilji was in the service of the sultan of Delhi, a Muslim ruler in northern India. Khilji defeated the armies of the Sena dynasty and conquered Bengal. The population had resisted Hindu caste beliefs and so quickly converted to casteless Islam, which emerged as the dominant religion of eastern Bengal. The region paid a regular tribute in war elephants to the Delhi sultanate (reign of the sultan), in exchange for a measure of self-rule. Khilji imposed a new administration on Bengal from his new capital in the town of Gaur. The region was divided into *iqta*, or districts, over which he appointed loyal generals as *muqtas* (governors and tax collectors). He ordered the building of mosques and madrassas, schools where the young studied the Islamic faith. Settlers arrived from Persia (modern Iran), central Asia, and the Middle East. They introduced new forms of art and architecture and transformed the culture of the region.

The reign of Bakhtiar Khilji ended a year after it began, however. He was killed by Ali Mardan Khalji, one of his lieutenants. With the support of the sultan of Delhi, Ali Mardan took control of Bengal and, in 1210, declared independence. He was a cruel and ambitious ruler. He inspired fierce hatred among the landowners and nobles of Bengal, who conspired to assassinate him in 1212.

During the early fourteenth century, a series of local dynasties emerged in Bengal. A Persian aristocrat, Ilias Shah, established a unified and independent state at the start of his reign in 1342. In the 1350s, Shah marched to Nepal. He brought the first Muslims to that region, as well as to eastern Bengal. The sultan of Delhi made an alliance with Bengal, which he recognized as an independent state.

The Shah dynasty included the reigns of Sikander (1358–1390) and Ghiyasuddin Azam (1390–1411). The Hindu faith thrived under a king named Ganesha, who took power in 1414. But the Muslim sultanate returned under Nasiruddin Mahmud in 1435. The Shah dynasty raised impressive new mosques and palaces. It patronized skilled Bengali writers, who developed a Bengali national literature. The region enjoyed stability and rising prosperity. Bengal flourished through trade with Southeast Asia and India.

In 1534 an ethnic Afghan warlord from India, Sher Shah Suri, invaded Bengal. He established an independent state in defiance of the sultan Humayun, who reigned in Delhi. In 1539 Humayun brought a powerful army to Bengal, intending to defeat Sher Shah Suri and force Bengal to submit to his authority. The armies of the two leaders clashed at the Battle of Chausa, where Humayun was totally defeated. Sher Shah Suri marched to Delhi and overthrew Humayun's government in 1540. He reformed the military and the administration of the sultanate. He set about making changes to the realm. He built a new system of roads and introduced the rupee coin as the standard currency throughout the realm. A system of taxes on trade goods provided money for the central treasury.

THE TIGER KING

Sher Shah Suri earned the name Sher Khan (king of the lions) as a young man after he killed a tiger. Later, his exploits in defeating the sultan of Delhi won Sher Khan a reputation as a great warrior. In the late nineteenth century, a Pashtun (Afghan) prince adopted the title for himself. The British author Rudyard Kipling, after meeting this prince, used the name for the ferocious human-eating tiger that appeared in his story collection *The Jungle Book*, which was published in 1894.

A young Muslim prince named Akbar took up many of these reforms and innovations. Akbar founded the Mughal Empire of northern India in the sixteenth century. The Mughal realm conquered the lower Ganges River plain in 1576. Under its new administration in Bengal, the sultan appointed nawabs, or governors, and zamindars, who collected rents and taxes from the farmers. The nawabs limited the power of wealthy landlords and levied a tax, known as the *jizya*, on all non-Muslim men. Under Mughal rule, Dhaka grew into an important city and eventually the realm's capital. The surrounding region exported a bounty of rice, silk, and sugarcane.

Mughal Rulers and the East India Company

European interest and influence in Asia had grown steadily over the fifteenth and sixteenth centuries. European trading companies built a post in Dhaka, where they bought silk and other goods for transport to Europe. French, Dutch, and British merchants seeking to open trade with India followed. But local landowners and the Mughal sultans opposed them. In 1632 a large force of Portuguese and their allies lost to a Bengali army at the Battle of Hoogly. The influence of the Portuguese in Bengal steadily declined after this.

As Portuguese influence waned, that of Great Britain grew stronger. British merchants formed the East India Company to bypass the Arab middlemen who controlled trade between the East Indies, a source of valuable spices, and Europe. The company built trading posts in Dhaka and bought the city of Kolkata (also known as Calcutta) from the nawab of Dhaka. But the Mughal sultan Aurangzeb, who came to power in 1658, opposed the British presence. The British and Mughal armies clashed in the 1680s. The nawab Shaista Khan also turned against the British, banning the East India Company from trading in Bengal.

Nonetheless, the British presence in the region grew. The authority of the Mughal rulers, who had their seat of power in distant Delhi, began to decline. Aurangzeb fought several major wars against neighboring states. He spent much of his reign putting down rebellions within the empire. The constant state of war weakened the empire. After Aurangzeb's death in 1707, the Mughal Empire began to break apart. That left an opening for the British. In 1717 the Mughal Empire began granting trade permits, known as *dastaks*, to British merchants. The merchants used these permits to avoid paying duties and taxes on their goods to the nawab of Bengal. The British also interfered in the court of Siraj-ud-Daulah, the nawab of Bengal. They supported opponents of the nawab to advance their economic and political control.

By the 1750s, the British were gathering their forces at Fort William in Kolkata. They were seeking to consolidate their control of Bengal. In early 1757, the nawab ordered his forces to capture the fort. After a surprise attack defeated the nawab's forces, the two sides signed a truce known as the Treaty of Alinagar. The British had secretly worked to overthrow Siraj-ud-Daulah, however. They promoted his rival, Mir Jafar, an Arab general in the nawab's army, as the new nawab.

On June 23, the nawab broke the truce and attacked the British forces in their camp at Plassey. Superior British guns turned the battle against Siraj-ud-Daulah, who lost several hundred soldiers and ordered a retreat. A week later, the British captured Siraj-ud-Daulah and made Mir Jafar the new nawab of Bengal.

After this victory, the British reinforced their influence in Bengal. They expelled their European competitors, including the Dutch and French. They founded an administrative system based on Great Britain's home government. Mir Jafar, however, resisted British control of his court and army. He allied with the Dutch East India Company, an organization founded in the Netherlands to exploit the spice trade in the East Indies. The Dutch merchants sent a small fleet to attack Fort William. After the British defeated this fleet, Mir Jafar fell from power. His son-in-law Mir Kasim replaced him and proved even less cooperative with the British.

In 1764 Mir Kasim's forces joined with those of the Mughal emperor Shah Alam II. They faced the British at the Battle of Buxar along the Ganges River in the Bihar region of India. Mir Kasim was defeated. The British victory gave the them direct political control of Bengal and northern India.

In this engraving from the eighteenth century, **Mughal emperor Shah Alam (right)** meets with Robert Clive of the East India Company.

The arrival of the British brought important social and political changes to Bengal. As the Mughal regime weakened, the Muslim administrators found their authority shrinking. The British set up new judicial and tax systems. They appointed Europeans as governors and administrators, keeping Bengali Muslims only in lower posts. The British also claimed the taxes, tolls, and fees that had been collected by the zamindars. The British forced the transfer of property from Muslim to Hindu landlords, raising resentment between the two communities. The British also disbanded the Mughal army and brought Bengali soldiers into the service of the East India Company.

With the consent of the company, Christian missionaries began arriving in Bengal in the early nineteenth century. The British banned traditional Muslim and Hindu religious practices that they considered uncivilized (for example, the Hindu custom of suttee, in which a wife is willingly cremated on the funeral pyre, or fire, of her husband). A judicial system based on British law replaced traditional Muslim courts. English became the language of administration and the new public schools.

Under British control, eastern Bengal produced mainly silk, rice, and jute for export. The East India Company organized irrigation works, built new roads, and linked the region to the rest of India by the first railroads. But as the population grew, very little manufacturing developed that would support a large urban population. The British did not want to create competition for industries in the British Isles. As a result, the weaving industry, a mainstay of the region's economy, nearly disappeared. In the countryside, the population began to exceed the soil and water resources. Vulnerable to poor growing seasons and monsoon floods, Bengal began to experience overcrowding and famine.

◉ Resistance against the British

In the early nineteenth century, the highest ranks of Indian society grew unhappy with British domination. Indian princes protested the British custom of seizing land and titles from local rulers who died without heirs. In addition, sepoys—Indian soldiers in the British army—saw their lifestyle and religious beliefs threatened by their foreign officers. Meanwhile, the British government sought to control the East India Company, which often was at odds with British foreign policy. In 1813 Great Britain's lawmakers ended the company's monopoly. In 1834 they made the company part of the British government.

These measures did not satisfy the sepoys. They began a violent uprising in 1857. Fighting at a military base near Kolkata quickly spread throughout northern and central India. After the British put down the Sepoy Rebellion, the government dissolved the East India Company. The British took direct control of Bengal.

Villagers stand near their **thatched huts on the Ganges River** in central Bangladesh in 1895. The British allowed Europeans—but not Bengalis—to buy land in the nineteenth century.

At this time, British control extended from eastern Bengal, across the entire Ganges plain, to the Indus River valley, in distant north-western India. The British let European farmers buy good land in the region, purposely excluding Bengalis. The British also moved into the Chittagong Hills. There British officials governed the local hill peoples, who had remained independent in their remote corner of eastern Bengal.

At the end of the nineteenth century, rivalry between Hindu and Muslim factions (groups) in Bengal increased. Hindus made up a majority of landlords and business investors. Meanwhile, most Muslims worked as landless farmers, with much less influence in the administration of the region. The British set up separate elections for Hindu and Muslim voters, which increased friction between the two groups. To fight for further independence from British rule, the elite members of the Hindu community formed the Indian National Congress in 1885. Muslims under the leadership of Syed Ahmed Khan opposed the organization. Khan believed that Muslims would benefit by full cooperation with the British and the promotion of English-language education.

In 1905 the British responded to these conflicting views by dividing Bengal. They set up a new administrative center for East Bengal in Dhaka. This division angered many Bengalis. They saw it as a challenge to their long tradition as a unified region. British control of local industries and agriculture still rankled as well.

In 1906 the Muslims of British India met in Dhaka to form the All-India Muslim League. This organization sought to protect the rights of Muslims, who made up about 20 percent of the population. The Indian nationalist movement, led by the Hindu majority, sought instead a unified and sovereign Indian nation. They believed the British were dividing the population to control it more easily. In the face of rising opposition to colonial rule, the British ended the division of Bengal in 1912.

World War II and Independence

India remained under the control of a British governor through the 1930s. A movement of noncooperation with British rule undertaken by Mohandas Gandhi—called the Mahatma, or "Great Soul"—began a period of more open hostility to British rule. Workers held strikes at mines and factories. Shops closed for business. Mass public meetings protested British actions.

In 1939 World War II (1939–1945) broke out between Great Britain and Germany in Europe. The British-led government of India declared India's support for Great Britain's effort—without consulting the people of India. In 1940 the Muslim League held a meeting in Lahore, in present-day Pakistan. There, they adopted the Lahore Resolution. It called for a new state to be formed in northwestern and eastern India—areas where Muslims formed a majority of the population.

In 1941 Germany's ally Japan attacked British bases in Malaysia and Burma (modern Myanmar). In December, Japan's surprise attack on a U.S. naval base at Pearl Harbor, Hawaii, prompted the United States to declare war on Japan. The war disrupted trade and further impoverished Bengal. In 1943 a terrible monsoon struck the region. It caused a famine that killed millions of people in the Ganges delta region.

World War II ended with the surrender of Germany in May 1945 and Japan in September 1945. Although Great Britain and its allies had won the war, it was left weakened and unable to hold on to its empire. India was one of its many colonies demanding independence.

In 1947 the British government granted independence to India. It partitioned the land into India and Pakistan, with the latter to be a largely Muslim nation. Bengal was divided into West Bengal, a province of India, and East Bengal, which became part of Pakistan. East Bengal was later named East Pakistan, with its capital at Dhaka. The separation of India and the two halves of Pakistan brought anarchy. Masses of Hindus and Muslims uprooted their families and moved across the borders. Many Hindus moved west into India. Muslims from the Indian states of Assam, Bihar, and Punjab streamed into East Pakistan. Although this eastern part of Pakistan held a larger population, the national government in West Pakistan dominated the country. It gave little attention to the interests and problems of the Bengalis.

East and West Pakistan were separated by hundreds of miles as well as by language and culture. In West Pakistan, the main language was Urdu. The leaders of Pakistan sought to unify their nation by imposing this language in East Pakistan, where for many centuries the people had spoken Bangla (also known as Bengali). Using a different vocabulary and written in an unfamiliar script, Urdu was foreign and unwelcome to the people of eastern Bengal.

Riots soon broke out in opposition to the language decree. The Bengali Language Movement organized many of these demonstrations, which caused friction between West and East Pakistan. An independence movement grew with the formation of the Awami League. On February 22, 1952, government forces confronted pro-Bengali students in Dhaka. The forces opened fire and killed several of the students. Modern Bangladesh marks this event each year as Martyrs' Day.

East Pakistan also found itself at an economic disadvantage. Most of its industries were under the control of investors and banks from West Pakistan. Discrimination against Bengali workers by outside managers led to a series of violent strikes in the jute mills of East Pakistan in the early 1950s.

In 1958 General Mohammad Ayub Khan took control of Pakistan. He imposed a military regime on the country. Khan declared himself president and won elections in 1965, although his opponents accused Khan and his allies of rigging the vote. In 1966 Khan ordered the arrest of Sheikh Mujibur Rahman (Mujib), the leader of the Awami League. The government tried Mujib in 1968 for conspiring with India to divide Pakistan. Mujib defended himself successfully and became a hero to the

The National Language Monument in Dhaka commemorates a protest on February 22, 1952, against Pakistan's attempt to impose the Urdu language on what later became Bangladesh. The police opened fire during the demonstration, killing several students.

An **Awami League leader** delivers a speech at a large rally in March 1970.

Pakistani Bengalis. In 1969 Khan resigned the presidency, partly due to unrest in the Pakistani army.

A devastating storm hit East Pakistan in 1970. It flooded most of the country, bringing disease and a dire lack of food. More than one million people died. The slow and poor response of the Pakistani government to this disaster inspired a stronger drive for independence. In 1971 Mujib led the Awami League to a sweeping victory in elections to the parliament (lawmaking body) of Pakistan, giving the party a legislative majority. The Pakistani government refused to recognize the results, however. In response, Mujib called for a rally at the Ramna Race Course in Dhaka. More than two million people arrived to hear the Awami League leader call for independence from Pakistan.

Agha Muhammad Yahya Khan, who had become the president on Ayub Khan's resignation, suspended the legislature. This action inspired Mujib to repeat his call for independence. In a symbolic declaration, the former East Pakistan adopted the name Bangladesh.

According to most accounts, the name Bangladesh comes from the Bang people. The Bang were a branch of the Dravidian people who settled the Indian subcontinent about 1000 B.C.

The Pakistani army then carried out a violent crackdown. Street battles between soldiers and civilians broke out in the streets of Dhaka and Chittagong. Demonstrators seized police stations, important crossroads, university campuses, and other strategic points. Mujib was arrested and brought to West Pakistan. Meanwhile, a group of guerrilla (independent, unconventional) freedom fighters, called the Mukhti Bahini, fought the Pakistani army. As a full-blown civil war erupted, millions of refugees fled the fighting.

The building tension finally broke in 1971. India invaded Bangladesh to help it gain independence. Heavy fighting between India and Pakistan broke out in Dhaka and other major cities. The Indo-Pakistani War of 1971 ended in Pakistan's swift defeat. On December 16, 1971, Pakistan formally surrendered. The brief war for independence had cost about three million lives.

East Pakistan won its independence as Bangladesh. The new nation set up a parliamentary democracy. Pakistan released Mujib, who returned to Bangladesh as the country's first prime minister. His Awami League became the dominant political party.

Members of the **Mukhti Bahini,** guerrilla freedom fighters, are pictured in the city of Khulna two days before East Pakistan declared independence and became Bangladesh in 1971.

Political Turmoil

Bangladesh suffered heavy damage during the war. The new country found itself struggling to support a rapidly growing population. In addition, an ethnic war broke out in the Chittagong region, as Bengali colonists moved in to seize land from the Chittagong hill tribes. The war continued for two decades, with full-scale battles fought between Chittagong guerrillas and the Bangladesh army causing thousands of deaths. Refugees streamed out of the region to shelter in camps in India and Burma.

Meanwhile, political factions within Bangladesh fought, often violently, for power. In 1975 Mujib banned opposition political parties, inspiring fierce resistance. Members of the army assassinated him later that year. In 1976 General Ziaur Rahman imposed a dictatorship and martial law (military rule) on the country. By rigging elections, Rahman arranged a loyal parliament that did his bidding. In 1978 he won the first presidential election in Bangladesh, while his Bangladesh Nationalist Party (BNP) rose to power.

In 1981 several army officers killed Rahman during an unsuccessful coup. Following a brief period of civilian rule, Bangladesh again came under military rule when General Hussain Muhammad Ershad staged a successful coup in 1982. The Jatiya Party (also called the National Party) formed to support Ershad. The new National Party won elections in 1986 and 1988. Opponents in the Awami League and the BNP boycotted (refused to participate in) these elections. They organized demonstrations to oppose Ershad and the National Party, leading to violence in the streets of Dhaka. Ershad dealt with any challenges to his authority with martial law, curfews, and imprisonment.

Meanwhile, Bangladesh made some economic progress. The country attracted foreign investment. New factories produced shoes, jute, and electronic goods. A revived garment industry employed a growing number of people in the cities. The country began building water-control projects in the countryside to help farmers cope with seasonal flooding.

Agricultural regions remained poor and vulnerable to seasons of high water and storms. In the spring of 1988, heavy snowmelt in the Himalayas flooded huge swaths of Bangladesh. The waters forced millions of rural people to take refuge in the cities. The floods destroyed

For links to websites on the history of Bangladesh and details on the current government, visit www.vgsbooks.com.

roads and railroads. They also forced the closing of the main airport in Dhaka, which hindered international relief efforts.

Facing fierce opposition and popular unrest, President Ershad resigned in 1990. A provisional (temporary) government came to power, with Shahabuddin Ahmed as president. The parliament elected Khaleda Zia, the widow of Ziaur Rahman, as the prime minister. She was the first woman in the history of Bangladesh to hold

Khaleda Zia

this important post. Zia's most popular opponent was one of Mujib's daughters, Sheikh Hasina Wajed, who led the Awami League. The elections of 1996 gave the victory to the BNP, and Zia returned as prime minister. But suspicion of fraud stirred millions to protest the results. Zia resigned and the elections were repeated that summer, with the Awami League and Wajed winning. Zia returned to power in 2001, while the office of president went to Iajuddin Ahmed, a former teacher. Ahmed, a political independent, won the office by being the only candidate to run.

Meanwhile, a radical Islamic group known as the Jama'atul Mujahideen Bangladesh (JMB) had formed in the Jamalpur district. The group called for the establishment of an Islamic state, to be governed by strict religious law. Drawing support from religious organizations in the Middle East, the JMB gained members in the northern half of Bangladesh and began carrying out bombings starting in 2002. Although the government has killed or captured several key JMB leaders, the group has survived. It has also made ties with Jamaat-i-Islami, a conservative Islamic political party.

Sheikh Hasina Wajed (right) stands with her father, Mujib, in 1970. Wajed led the Awami League in the 1990s.

HUMAN CHAIN

On December 11, 2004, to protest against the government run by its rivals, the Awami League asked its supporters to come out to form a human chain. More than five million people answered the call. They joined arms across a distance of 652 miles (1,050 km). The chain stretched from Teknaf, near Myanmar, to Tentulia, on the border with India in northern Bangladesh. It was the longest human chain in history.

◎ Recent Events

Through three decades of independence, the governments of Bangladesh had failed to provide a growing economy and hope to millions of urban workers. In an attempt to attract foreign investment, the state had set up export processing zones (EPZs). Foreign companies within the EPZs operated with few restrictions and low taxes and duties on their goods. These zones did little to raise wages or benefit workers, however. In the spring of 2006, workers held strikes and protests against the poor working conditions. Protestors marched in the streets, blocked roads, and burned more than a dozen factories to the ground.

These textile riots continued throughout 2006. Working conditions weren't the only issue. Government corruption was also a point of friction. Since independence the nation's rival political parties had been unable to work together. The BNP and the Awami League acted as sworn enemies. Each had undermined the other with threats of violence and by rallying workers and militias (small, armed groups of civilians) to their cause. Through 2006 the Awami League protested the dominance of the BNP by boycotting the parliament, keeping its members from debating or voting on new laws. The political turmoil has encouraged the growth of new political parties, some of them dedicated to radical and violent means.

A new crisis emerged in early 2007. A caretaker government was holding power in preparation for scheduled elections, according to the constitution. In January, however, the Awami League announced a boycott of the elections. The league was protesting the possibility of fraud and the control of the election system by members of the BNP. President Ahmed canceled the elections. He announced a state of emergency, as rioting erupted in Dhaka. The cities came under a strict nighttime curfew, enforced by the police and the army.

Ahmed then stepped down from his post. His replacement, Fakhruddin Ahmed, took control of a provisional government that holds power under the close supervision of the Bangladeshi military, led by General

Moeen U Ahmed. The military has pledged to end corruption and return Bangladesh to civilian rule with new elections in 2008.

Fakhruddin Ahmed

⊙ Government

The constitution of 1972 set down the framework of the government of Bangladesh. All adults over the age of eighteen may vote to elect the members of the Jatiyo Sangshad, the nation's parliament. The Jatiyo Sangshad is made up of more than three hundred members serving five-year terms. The number of members from each party depends on the overall percentage that party wins in the elections. In 2004 the legislature passed a law that requires women to make up a set percentage of members.

Every five years, the legislature elects the president. The president is the head of state and appoints the prime minister, who represents the party that has won a majority in parliament. The prime minister runs the government and selects the cabinet members (government advisers). The prime minister also serves a five-year term. At the end of this term, a caretaker government holds power for three months. In this system, adopted in 1996, the temporary government oversees elections and formally hands over power to the new leader. The caretaker system is designed to subdue political turmoil and lessen the risk of violent coups.

The Supreme Court is the highest court in the land. The prime minister selects the court members, while the president formally appoints them. By the constitution, the president has the power to appoint as many judges as needed to handle the business of the court. Lower courts handle criminal and civil cases, as well as family disputes.

Bangladesh inherited the system of English common law that was in effect in British India. Since independence the country has adopted new laws and legal customs. Sharia, for example, is Islamic law. It is enforced by courts run by Muslim scholars and religious leaders. Sharia courts deal with local disputes and matters such as marriage and divorce. Bangladesh allows each religious community to enforce its own customs in family law cases.

Bangladesh is made up of six large divisions: Dhaka, Chittagong, Sylhet, Rajshahi, Khulna, and Barisal. Each division is named after the city that serves as its capital. The nation is further divided into 64 districts, called *zila*. The zila are further divided into 493 subdistricts (*upazila).*

THE PEOPLE

The population of Bangladesh is more than 150 million. This makes it the seventh most populous country in the world—ahead of vastly larger nations such as Russia. Bangladeshis also live in the most densely populated nation on the planet, with an average of 2,681 people per square mile (1,035 per sq. km).

The population of Bangladesh is very young, with 60 percent of the population aged 25 or younger. The population grows fast, with 27 births and only 8 deaths each year per 1,000 people. If the current rate of 1.9 percent growth remains steady, the population of Bangladesh will reach 190 million by the year 2025.

More than 70 percent of Bangladeshis live in the countryside, in villages built along the streams and canals that irrigate crop fields and pastures. Villagers build their homes with a frame of steel rods or bamboo poles, using straw or bamboo matting for walls and sheets of steel for the roof. Since the danger of flooding is high, many homes are raised a few feet off the ground on stilts. More durable homes

are made with clay bricks or concrete blocks. In cities, apartment buildings house most of the population. Large shantytowns dot the outskirts, home to the poor and to new arrivals from the countryside. Many of these neighborhoods lack basic necessities such as sewage systems, freshwater, and electricity.

Since the 1950s, the urban population has been growing rapidly. The overcrowding in the countryside forced millions of village dwellers to move to the cities. Dhaka and other cities spread across the nearby countryside as the new arrivals built makeshift shelters. These neighborhoods eventually developed into large slum areas poorly served by basic necessities.

◉ Ethnic Groups

About 98 percent of the nation's people are ethnic Bengalis. They share a common language, culture, and ancestry. The Bengalis trace their origins to the Bang tribe, which migrated to the Ganges delta region

This girl is a member of **the Jumma,** a people in southeastern Bangladesh who are mainly Buddhists.

about 1000 B.C. The majority of modern Bengalis are Muslim. Their dialect of the Bangla language differs from that spoken in West Bengal, India.

A group of hill tribes in the Chittagong region, known as the Jumma, make up about 2 percent of Bangladesh's population. The Jumma include smaller groups such as the Chakma, Marma, and Tripura. These ethnic groups are related to people of neighboring Myanmar. Many of them follow the Buddhist faith. They migrate from one place to another in search of good land. Using the slash-and-burn method, they make clearings in the forest cover. The Jumma and ethnic Bengalis have clashed over the years as they competed for land.

A handful of other ethnic groups live in Bangladesh, with their numbers being very small. Some people of Indian descent have migrated from the Indian states of West Bengal, Assam, and Bihar into Bangladesh. In addition, some Muslims from Myanmar have arrived as refugees in Bangladesh, fleeing conflict in their own country.

Language

For Bangladeshis, ethnic and national identity begins with their official language, Bengali. Known among its speakers as Bangla, this language is part of the Indo-Aryan language family. Bengali is related to Pali—a historic language of Buddhism—as well as to languages spoken in eastern India. Bengali is written in letters derived from Sanskrit, an ancient writing system native to the Indian subcontinent. Written from left to right, the script includes symbols for fifty letters.

Bengali comes in two main forms. Sadhubhasa is the formal, literary form. It is most common in poetry and songs. Chaltibhasa is the spoken everyday form. It is simpler and more flexible and even borrows some of its words from foreign tongues.

Bengali is a source of pride to many Bangladeshis. They associate the language with their hard-won independence. During the 1950s, students staged large demonstrations to oppose the forced use of Urdu, a Pakistani language. Several people were killed by police, an event still honored each year on February 21 as Language Movement Day, or Martyrs' Day.

British colonization brought the English language to Bengal. University courses are often taught in English. It has become an important second language for scholarship, the media, and business. Several major newspapers are published in English, and some radio stations broadcast in this tongue. Many street and shop signs in the cities of Bangladesh display their information in both Bengali and English.

◐ Women and Families

Traditionally, women have held second-class status in Bangladesh. Girls usually receive less schooling than boys. They are expected to marry at a young age. Professional matchmakers or male relatives arrange marriages in many families. Young single women feel intense pressure to marry, rather than pursue higher education or a career. Once they have their own household, women are expected to take most of the responsibility for rearing children.

Women follow a strictly defined role in many rural areas of Bangladesh. By long tradition, they keep to the home and its surroundings. While men work in the fields, women carry out the heavy work of drawing water, threshing grain, weaving, making pottery, and maintaining the home. Few of them have the help of electricity and appliances. Even in urban areas, women generally have less education than men. But attitudes

MARRIAGE CUSTOMS

Among both Hindus and Muslims, the payment of a bride-price and a dowry are customary when a couple is engaged to be married. A dowry is a sum paid to the groom's family by the father of the bride. For the bride-price, the groom and his family agree on a sum of money and gold jewelry to be paid to the family of the bride. The groom presents the gold on the day of the wedding. Many Bangladeshi women wear gold bracelets, rings, and other ornaments. In some cases, these pieces represent their bride-price as well as their family's savings.

This **woman sells her pottery** in a small village outside of Cox's Bazaar in Bangladesh. Many households survive by selling simple, handmade goods such as pottery, mats, baskets, and furniture.

MICRO BIZ

Despite traditional barriers, many women in Bangladesh have managed to start their own businesses. The new trend in microcredit has helped them. Banks in Bangladesh lend them small sums for equipment and materials. The women set up looms or other craft businesses in their homes or nearby workshops. They sell their wares in local markets. This trend has helped many women and families in Bangladesh out of dire poverty.

are slowly changing, due in part to the contributions from leaders such as Khaleda Zia and Sheikh Hasina Wajed. As a result, the ranks of women doctors, lawyers, politicians, and teachers are gradually growing.

Households in Bangladesh include an extended family of unmarried children as well as married sons. After puberty, boys and girls are separated. Parents instruct them in their proper adult roles as husbands and wives. In many families, the wife's role is limited and strictly defined. Husbands discourage women from leaving the home or seeking a job.

Health

Overcrowding, poor sanitation, and a lack of medical facilities—especially in rural areas—all affect the condition of public health in Bangladesh. The nation is growing rapidly. Families are large, and women, on average, have six children during their lifetime. Life expectancy in Bangladesh stands at 62 years (62 years for men and 63 years for women). These figures are typical of countries in the region.

Bangladesh has suffered many disease epidemics caused by poor sanitation and unclean water. A digestive infection called cholera has been a threat since ancient times, especially in crowded urban areas. Mosquitoes carry dengue fever and malaria. These diseases, combined with poor nutrition, challenge the nation's medical system.

In times of monsoon flooding, malnutrition (poor nutrition) is widespread, especially among the very young. This weakens the immune system, making people further vulnerable to disease. About 43 percent of all children under the age of five are underweight, a percentage that is the fifth-highest in the world. The rate of infant mortality stands at 65 deaths per 1,000 births, a high rate among the nations of south Asia. Bangladesh has greatly reduced this rate since 2000 through immunization (shots to prevent disease). These programs protect infants from measles, which was once epidemic among the young.

To improve public health, the government of Bangladesh has taken some steps, including inoculation (shots to strengthen the immune

SENSE OF HUMOR

A healing system known as the *unani* is common in Bangladesh. Healers, called hakims, treat illnesses, wounds, insect stings, infections, and other problems. The hakim relies on the idea of the four humors: blood, phlegm, yellow bile, and black bile—a system developed by the ancient Greeks. A healthy person is supposed to have a balance of the four humors. Disease results from an imbalance.

The hakim diagnoses the condition of the patient by measuring the speed, rhythm, and intensity of the pulse. Treatments come in many different forms. Special diets, exercise, and the use of herbs are common. Other treatments include massage, cauterization (burning), and purging (forcing out the contents of the stomach). Cupping is another treatment. Hakims place small cups on the body. They heat the cups to create suction. The treatment is supposed to draw out certain humors to restore the balance.

In a country where clinics and medicines are in short supply, many people turn to the unani system.

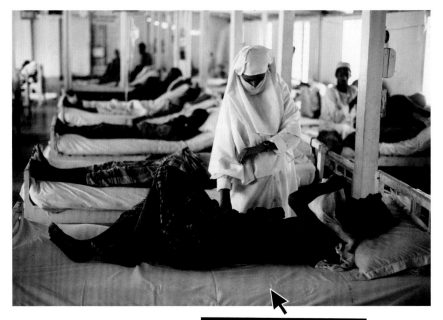

A nurse checks a malaria patient in **a hospital in rural Bangladesh.** Health care in Bangladesh is being improved with help from foreign aid organizations.

system against certain diseases). This program has all but eliminated polio, a dangerous childhood disease. Foreign aid organizations have built medical clinics and brought in trained health-care workers. Bangladesh also has largely escaped the epidemic of HIV-AIDS (human immunodeficiency virus and acquired immunodeficiency syndrome). Less than 0.1 percent of the population carries the HIV virus that causes AIDS.

The nation has also had great success battling tuberculosis. Each year, about 300,000 Bangladeshis contract the disease, which attacks the lungs and other bodily systems. An organization called the Bangladesh Rural Advancement Committee (BRAC) runs treatment centers, where people can receive immunizations as well as crucial antibiotics, which have a cure rate of more than 95 percent. In the past, a big problem has been that patients don't finish their course of antibiotics, leading to new, drug-resistant strains of the disease. But in this program, patients must pay an amount equal to about $5, which they get back if they complete the six-month course of antibiotics.

To learn more about the most current health statistics for Bangladesh, go to www.vgsbooks.com for links.

◉ Education

Bangladesh requires children to attend school for eight years. Primary school lasts for five years, starting at the age of six. Despite the law, about 5 percent of the nation's children don't attend primary school at all. Others attend sporadically. Most of these children stay home to work in small workshops, a family industry, or on a farm.

Secondary school runs for seven years, with three years of attendance required by law. About 48 percent of children eligible for secondary school actually attend. Most secondary schools are private and charge fees to students. A big difference exists in education levels among men and women. The literacy rate in Bangladesh has reached about 50 percent for men and 31 percent for women, though this rate is probably much higher among the young.

Bangladesh has thirteen universities and technical institutes. The largest is the University of Dhaka in the capital city. Chittagong and Rajshahi also have major universities. Students seeking a professional degree attend engineering schools, agriculture schools, medical schools, and an institute of Islamic studies for religious scholars.

These **girls show signs with their names** at a girls high school in Chittagong.

CULTURAL LIFE

Bengal has long been a cultural center of south Asia. It has a complex political history, many different religious traditions, and a rich literature. From a young age, the people of Bangladesh are familiar with famous works of music and poetry, traditional modes of dress and conduct, and family customs that are a part of this centuries-old Bengali culture.

◯ Religion

About 83 percent of people in Bangladesh are Muslims, mainly of the Sunni sect. The faith of Islam arrived in Bangladesh during invasions in the 1200s and 1300s. In 1947 Hindu and Muslim populations of India were separated by the establishment of Pakistan. This event set off a mass migration of people across the borders. It also triggered deadly violence between the two groups.

Muslims follow the teachings of the prophet Muhammad, who founded the faith on the Arabian Peninsula in the seventh century.

Muslims believe that Allah (Arabic for "God") revealed his teachings to Muhammad. These revelations are collected in the Quran. The deeds and sayings of Muhammad are collected in the Hadith. Together, the books provide spiritual, political, and legal guides to believers. A mystical Islamic sect known as the Sufis also thrives in Bangladesh. Members of this sect try to experience God directly through rituals.

All Muslims have a duty to follow the Five Pillars of Islam. These duties are declaring faith in Allah and his prophet Muhammad, daily prayer, giving alms (offerings to the poor), and fasting from food and water during the holy month of Ramadan. They also must make a pilgrimage to the holy city of Mecca, Saudi Arabia, at least once, if possible.

Hindus make up about 16 percent of the population. Hinduism derives from the ancient Vedic culture. Hindus have a variety of spirits, gods, and beliefs they apply to their daily lives. Hindu doctrines include samsara (reincarnation) and karma (the spiritual consequences of one's actions). Many Hindu families have small shrines in their

MADRASSA EDUCATION

The madrassa is a traditional Muslim school. In many places in Bangladesh, madrassas serve as the most important primary school for boys and girls. After the arrival of Islam in Bangladesh, madrassas taught a wide range of fields, including grammar, logic, law studies, philosophy, and divinity. Under rule by the East India Company, many madrassas were closed down. Others were changed to train students for service in the colonial government. In madrassas throughout Bengal, students had to learn English. In modern times, by the government's official count, twelve thousand madrassas operate in Bangladesh. Combined, they have about 3.5 million students. A government ministry oversees the schools, while a teacher-training institute prepares instructors.

homes. They carry out rituals of purification each day and make regular visits to local temples. There they offer food and other goods to the gods and seek to carry out worthy actions that will earn them spiritual merit.

Other religions claim about 1 percent of the population as followers. Christians—most of them Roman Catholic—arrived with European settlers, including the Portuguese and British, who established missions in the region. Christian missionaries converted some local peoples to their faith.

Buddhism, meanwhile, has a long history in the region. The nation has several historic Buddhist shrines and monasteries. Buddhism has thrived in the Chittagong region, whose people resisted the Muslim invasion of the lowlands and control by the Islamic Mughal emperors. In Buddhist families, young men may enter a monastery for a short time to study Buddhist scriptures and lead a devout and humble life.

The government of Bangladesh is secular (not based on religion), and the constitution of Bangladesh calls for the freedom of religion. Nevertheless, Buddhists, Christians, and Hindus experience some discrimination in education and in government service. In addition, the government has passed laws against certain books of the Ahmadiyya sect, a branch of Islam. The followers of this faith differ from other Islamic sects in some key tenets of the faith.

Literature

A tradition of Bengali poetry, stories, religious tracts, and novels stretches back more than one thousand years. The *Charyapada* of the eighth century, a collection of hymns dedicated to the Buddha, is the earliest known work in the Bengali language. Soon after, writers composed religious songs and poetry, and lessons to educate the faithful.

In the nineteenth century, the educator Vidyasagar wrote grammar books and translated Sanskrit works into Bengali, ushering in the era of modern Bengali literature.

The Bengali renaissance, or rebirth, was a movement of famous writers who spoke out against British dominance of Bengal's society and culture. The movement began with the works of Dinabandhu Mitra. In 1860 Mitra wrote the play *The Indigo Mirror* to celebrate the role East Bengal played in the Sepoy Rebellion of 1857.

The world-famous Rabindranath Tagore took up the movement. A prolific writer and composer, Tagore composed more than two thousand songs known as Rabindra Sangeet. He also wrote short stories, novels, and poems. In 1913 he became the first Asian to win a Nobel Prize in Literature, for his contribution to world literature. Tagore remains a revered figure in India and Bangladesh. Both countries adopted national anthems from his works.

Rabindranath Tagore

Kazi Nazrul Islam was another key Bengali poet. He led the effort to throw off British rule by writing thousands of defiant poems and songs. Many of these songs were taken up by the people of East Pakistan in their fight for independence in 1971.

Drama also has a rich tradition in Bangladesh. *Jatra* performances take place on open-air stages in towns throughout the country. This style originated centuries ago and developed into a major entertainment form. Jatra shows can last for several hours or all night long. They include music, dancing, comic sketches, and epic tales of heroism and romance.

Taslima Nasrin

One of the best-known modern Bangladeshi writers is Taslima Nasrin. Nasrin often writes on the role of women in Bangladesh society. She speaks out against some of the unfair traditions of Bangladesh, drawing the anger of critics. Her opinions are often very unpopular among some Bangladeshis. For this reason, she has lived in Europe since the 1990s.

◉ Media

The people of Bangladesh have a choice of about two hundred daily newspapers. *Prothom Alo* (First Light) is the most widely circulated. National papers are printed in Dhaka, while various regional papers are published in other major cities. However, regular readership is low—about 15 percent of the population. English-language papers include the *Daily Star*, the *Bangladesh Observer*, and *Bangladesh Today*.

Bangladeshis listen to a variety of programs on Bangladesh Betar, the government-controlled radio network. This system has local stations in Dhaka, Chittagong, Khulna, and other large cities. It also broadcasts on a shortwave (long-range) channel that reaches Bengali speakers throughout south Asia and the Middle East. The British Broadcasting Corporation (BBC) and the Voice of America also broadcast in Bengali. Bangladesh Television (BTV) broadcasts throughout the country during the daytime. In the twenty-first century, the number of privately owned channels broadcasting via satellite has grown.

The government closely monitors films, books, television programs, magazines, and newspapers. A censorship bureau watches for any material critical of the government or for anything it deems indecent, slanderous, or obscene. Protests against government policy or national leaders, for example, may be censored. The bureau has banned films, taken television stations off the air, and prohibited certain books. It also issues censorship guidelines for writers, journalists, and film directors.

Visit www.vgsbooks.com for links to websites with additional information about music, films, books, and television programs in Bangladesh.

Music

Bangladesh has a great variety of Bengali folk music styles. Many of them feature solo singers. Others add string and drum instruments. Every region of the country has different musical traditions. *Gombhira*, for example, is a northern tradition in which the music is sung and danced by two performers.

Skilled musicians take many years to master the sitar, a stringed instrument that is important in the classical music of India. Its music is based on the raga, a form that allows the performer to improvise on a certain scale of notes. Hundreds of different raga forms exist. Each form is played to evoke a certain emotion.

Baul is a popular genre of singing that dates back centuries. Baul is inspired by the Sufi, a mystical Islamic sect, and is often performed by hermits who travel from village to village. They are accompanied by the

This musician plays **drums and the sitar (right)** at a hotel in Dhaka.

ektara, a simple stringed instrument, or the multi-stringed *dotara*. Baul musicians also use simple flutes, cymbals, and hide-covered drums.

Songs written by Rabindranath Tagore have a musical tradition of their own, known as Rabindra Sangeet. Many performers specialize in the more than two thousand works of this style, which expresses a wide range of emotions and themes. The leading performers of Rabindra Sangeet include Pankaj Mullick, Debabrata Biswas, and Kanika Bandyopadhyay.

Festivals and Holidays

Bangladeshis enjoy festivals throughout the year, as well as a calendar full of public holidays. February 21 is Language Movement Day. This day marks the violent resistance to the imposition of the Urdu language in the 1950s. Independence Day is celebrated on March 26. It marks the day on which Bangladesh proclaimed its name and freedom from Pakistan. December 16 is Victory Day. On that day, Pakistan's military leaders surrendered to Bangladesh and India in 1971.

Pahela Baishakh, a traditional New Year's Day celebration, takes place on April 14. (The new year begins in the spring because the old Bangladeshi calander followed the growing seasons). On this day, great public fairs take place, with entire cities meeting in the street for processions, tournaments, and races. Nobanno is the nation's harvest day, taking place in November or December. Farming families bring in their crop of new rice and prepare cakes and dishes of sweet milk and rice. The festival of Poush in January is a traditional winter festival.

During the monthlong fast of Ramadan, also known as Roza in

Children in Dhaka take part in a **Hindu celebration** observing the day the Hindu god Lord Krishna was born.

Muslim boys exchange greetings during a religious festival at a mosque in Dhaka.

Bangladesh, Muslims refrain from eating or drinking during the daylight hours. Eid al-Fitr is a celebration feast that ends the fast of Ramadan. Muslims also observe Eid al-Adha, when they follow the custom of slaughtering a sheep and giving food to the poor. The Birth of Muhammad is another important holiday. Islamic holidays follow a lunar (moon) calendar, so holidays change dates and even seasons over time.

Buddhists, Hindus, and Christians have holidays of their own. Buddha Purnima is the Buddha's birthday, a holiday that arrives with the full moon in the fourth month of the lunar calendar. A major Hindu festival is Durga Puja, a time of worship. Christmas in Bangladesh is known as the Great Day, or Borodin.

Sports

Bangladesh takes great pride in the Tigers, its international cricket team. Cricket is a bat-and-ball sport somewhat similar to baseball. The team takes part in international championships known as test matches. In the 2007 Cricket World Cup, Bangladesh defeated teams from India and South Africa. Bangladeshis also enjoy soccer (football), tennis, badminton, and field hockey. Bangladesh has sent athletes to the Olympic Games as well as the Asian Games and the Commonwealth Games, organized by former members of the British Empire.

At the 2006 Asian Games, the Bangladesh *kabaddi* team won a bronze medal. A traditional team sport, kabaddi is played by two teams with seven members. The teams take sides on a small court, with members of one team crossing to the other side to tag opposing team members. Kabaddi demands quickness and good stamina, as players are not supposed to take a breath while in enemy territory.

Sports clubs play an important role in athletic training and competition. City governments, military branches, universities, and private companies all have sports clubs. Many accept young people just learning to compete, while also fielding teams in soccer, cricket, kabaddi, basketball, and volleyball leagues. Sports clubs also train handball, badminton, and tennis players. Some are open to competition in board games such as chess and backgammon.

Arts and Crafts

Bangladesh is home to a great variety of craft traditions. Many arise from the making of basic household utensils, such as clay pots, glass jars and vases, and woven mats. The elaborate stitching of *nakshi kantha*, or cloth embroidery, decorates bedspreads, pillowcases, and quilts. The same elaborate designs often appear in *nakshi pitha*, or cake decoration.

Bangladeshis fashion jewelry and ornaments from gold, silver, and brass, using gemstones and pearls as inlay. Gold and silver also go into cosmetic jars and vases. Conch shells are also fashioned into jewelry or used for small jars, lamps, ashtrays, and paint pots. For many Bangladeshi families, much of the wealth of the household is in the form of gold rings, bracelets, earrings, and other small valuables that hold their value and are easy to keep. Woodworkers create furniture and musical instruments, often decorating their works with wood carvings.

Another popular craft is *patachitra*, long painted scrolls showing religious stories, fables, and historical scenes. The patachitra originated with the spread of Buddhism, which was explained in illustrated stories of the Buddha's life and teachings. Later, Hindus and Muslims also took up this form of storytelling.

Alpana drawings are made from a paste of crushed rice, with vermilion, yellow turmeric spice, ash, or crushed red brick used for coloring. The geometric designs of the alpana are associated with Hindu rites and holidays. The drawing is made with a finger or the tip of a stick and usually decorates the entrance to a home.

RICKSHAW ART

A common sight in cities is the brightly painted rickshaw (below), a two-wheeled cart that transports cargo or passengers. The heavy rain and high humidity of Bangladesh quickly fades the paint, so each year the backboard of a rickshaw is repainted. Rickshaw painters are trained professionals. They study with experienced artists to hone their trade. In some families, the skill is passed on from one generation to the next.

Different cities favor different art themes. In Dhaka, rickshaws often display movie stars and scenes. In Chittagong, nature scenes are common, as well as birds, flowers, and animals. In Sylhet, rickshaws are left plain and unpainted.

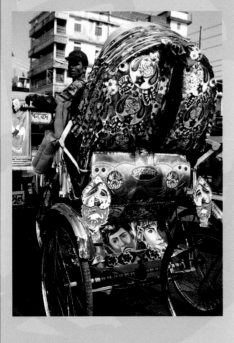

◉ Food

Food in Bangladesh has taken influences from India, Southeast Asia, and Great Britain. Meals and eating habits vary widely by location, religion, and economic status. For example, Muslims don't eat pork, while Hindus don't eat beef. Among the poor, meat may be reserved for special occasions. Rice is the basic staple of almost all of Bangladesh's people, especially the poor. It is prepared by frying with cooking oil or boiling in a pot of water.

Families may gather as often as four times during the day to eat and drink together. *Panthabat* is the morning meal. It often includes bread or rice and tea. A noon lunch often features fish. Tiffin, a late-afternoon teatime, includes tea and biscuits or cakes. The evening supper may offer rice, meat, cooked lentils known as dal, and a salad or dish of vegetables.

Bangladeshi food features a great variety of spices and flavors. Curry dishes are made with powdered spices that combine several ingredients—usually ginger, mint, cardamom, turmeric, and cinnamon. Curry often flavors chicken, mutton (sheep), beef, and fish. A plate of rice or lentils may accompany curry dishes. Mung beans, coconut, and mustard liven up curry and other dishes. *Kalia* is a favorite curry dish with meat and potatoes. Traditional *biryani* combines fried rice with mutton or chicken. Spicy dishes that came from Persia and central Asia include kebabs—lamb or mutton grilled on skewers—and *koftas* (spiced meatballs).

Fish in Bangladesh includes carp, catfish, and the hilsa—the national fish. These fish are cooked by steaming, frying, or boiling. Dried, smoked, and salted fish is a favorite treat. Shellfish, including shrimp, is also plentiful along the coasts.

Cooks prepare cakes and sweet milk dishes for dessert and holiday treats. The milky tea known as *cha* goes with every meal. Popular beverages include lassi (a yogurt drink), coconut water, and soft drinks. The most common fruit is the mango, which is abundant throughout south Asia. Papayas, jackfruit, watermelon, coconuts, oranges, bananas, pineapples, apricots, and lychees are also popular.

PINEAPPLE CHUTNEY

Chutney is a spicy condiment that originated in India and is popular in Bangladesh and all over south Asia. It goes with cooked meats as a sauce or, as a side dish, with bread, rice, crackers, or raw vegetables. Most types of chutney are made with chopped-up fruit, vinegar or lime juice, spices, and sugar. This is a type of pineapple chutney.

1 tablespoon vegetable oil

2 green chilies (adjust to taste), seeded and chopped

1 teaspoon *panch phoron* (optional, a seed mixture that can be bought in Indian or Asian grocery stores)

2 medium pineapples, peeled, cored, and chopped, bite sized, or 2 large cans of chopped pineapple

1 cup dried dates or apricots, finely chopped

1 2-inch piece of gingerroot, peeled and grated

1 cup sugar

1 teaspoon salt

1 tablespoon lime juice

1. Heat oil in a large frying pan. Add the chilies and the panch phoron (optional). Sauté 3 to 4 minutes.
2. Add the pineapple and heat on medium heat.
3. Add chopped dates or apricots, grated ginger, sugar, and salt. Mix well.
4. Cook on low heat until the pineapple cubes are soft, about 15 minutes. Stir occasionally.
5. Add lime juice when cooked. Use as a sauce for cooked meats or rice, or spread on warm bread or crackers. Keep any leftover chutney in the refrigerator.

Serves 10 or more

THE ECONOMY

Bangladesh has long struggled with overcrowding, a lack of resources and outside investment, and political turmoil. Its British rulers invested little in manufacturing. The workforce remained rural, unskilled, and poorly educated. The war of 1971 caused heavy damage. Monsoons and flooding have also forced the country to rebuild. Bangladesh has relied on international loans to develop new businesses. As a result, it has a heavy burden of foreign debt.

The nation is working to build a better future. Flood control projects limit the damage of monsoon flooding. The government also directs investment to rural villages, where millions of landless people find work in small factories. In the cities, foreign firms have invested in industries that make clothing, electronics, and other goods for export. Public projects such as roads, bridges, and power plants are also under way. These projects improve Bangladesh's infrastructure (public works) and provide jobs for unskilled laborers. They also help to modernize the nation and make it more appealing to foreign investors.

web enhanced @ www.vgsbooks.com

Bangladesh remains dependent on foreign aid and investment. This flow of money, however, rises and falls from year to year. In times of political violence and civil unrest, investment lessens. Corruption within the Bangladeshi government also discourages outside investment. Some groups, including labor unions, oppose legal reforms that would trim government services and allow more private companies to form and operate. As a result, the pace of economic reform remains slow.

Bangladesh is attempting to broaden its exports to include electronic goods, computer software, and other high-value products. This would lessen the country's heavy dependence on the textile industry. The effort to diversify industries and attract foreign investment has found some success. In 2007 the gross domestic product (GDP)—the yearly total value of all goods and services produced in a country—rose an estimated 4.5 percent from 2006. It was a promising sign for an economy badly in need of a boost.

BANKING FOR THE POOR

In 1983 Muhammad Yunus founded the Grameen Bank in Dhaka. The bank's purpose was to make small loans to the poor to help them start a business. The bank didn't ask for any collateral (property to guarantee the loan would be repaid). Instead, it asked borrowers to form groups of at least five people. This encouraged people to help one another in case of any financial trouble. If any member of the group failed to pay back a loan, the others in the group could not borrow anymore. The bank also encouraged borrowers to set up savings accounts.

The bank proved a success. By 2008 it had more than two thousand branches and had loaned about $5 billion to more than seven million people. Most of the loans went to poor women, many of whom had trouble finding employment or who stayed in their homes according to custom. Most of these women set up small workshops in their homes or began retail businesses. The microcredit industry started by the Grameen Bank has spread to other countries in Asia and around the world. In 2006 Yunus won a Nobel Prize for his work.

Services

Services provide about 52 percent of Bangladesh's GDP and employ 26 percent of the population. Service businesses include banking, insurance, real estate, retail stores, transportation, communications, and tourism. The public services sector is large and growing. It includes office workers, police, firefighters, health-care workers, railway workers, teachers, road builders, garbage collectors, and other workers.

The service sector has been growing rapidly as the economy of Bangladesh expands. The volume of goods traveling through the country's ports and via the road network is on the rise. The banking industry is involved in new investment in export businesses, as well as the microcredit business started by the Grameen Bank. In addition, the expansion of the mobile phone network and the Internet have all created new jobs and led to the founding of new high-tech service companies.

A young tourism industry holds promise as an important future source of income in Bangladesh. The nation's earnings from tourism are quite small. But tourism has been steadily rising. The country offers visitors historic sites, natural wonders such as the Sundarbans, and the long natural beach at Cox's Bazaar in the Chittagong region. Most visitors arrive from neighboring India. Bangladesh also draws tourists from the United Kingdom, the United States, Japan, South Korea, Pakistan, and China.

People gather on the **beach at Cox's Bazaar** in southeastern Bangladesh. The long beach is a tourist attraction.

Industry and Manufacturing

The industrial sector includes manufacturing, mining, and energy. It makes up about 28 percent of the GDP and employs about 11 percent of the workforce. Bangladesh is diversifying its industry. New investment has gone to steel, cement, shipbuilding, and automobile factories. A shipyard has opened at Khulna for repairing and rebuilding ships, and a steel mill operates in Chitt-agong. Foreign companies have helped the country develop a small electronics sector to make computer components and software.

Historically, Bengal was an important producer of textiles. This business remains a key industry of modern Bangladesh. The country grows or imports cotton and other raw materials to make cloth. It also finishes clothing for export around the world. Clothing factories employ many laborers in Dhaka and other major cities. Even in small villages, many families own small, hand-operated looms. They use the looms to produce clothing, rugs, scarves, tablecloths, and other woven goods that are then

Visit www.vgsbooks.com for links to websites with information about the textile industry in Bangladesh, including additional details about the factories in major cities and the villagers who produce textiles with their own looms.

This **tailor** works in the city of Chittagong. His sewing machine is set up on the street to do repairs and alterations.

sold by the piece to whole-sale buyers. Other cottage industries (small home businesses) in Bangladeshi villages make cigarettes from locally grown tobacco, bamboo furniture, carpets, and household pottery.

Bangladeshi companies also operate food-process-ing centers. These factories package the country's crops and prepare seafood for export. Jute mills turn out sacking material. Bangladesh also has fertilizer and chemical factories, sugar mills, glass factories, and aluminum works. Many of these plants depend on imported raw materials, however. When such resources become too expensive, the factories must operate at a loss or shut down.

The bamboo in the Chittagong Hills and the various softwood trees growing in the Sundarbans provide raw material for papermaking. The nation has paper mills at Chandraghona, Chhatak, and Paksey, as well as a paper and board mill at Khulna. Lumber mills make construction material, paper, cardboard, and newsprint.

Agriculture, Fishing, and Forestry

Agriculture (including fishing and forestry) generates 20 percent of Bangladesh's GDP. It employs 63 percent of the nation's workers. Farmers hold small plots of land, most between 1 and 4 acres (0.4 and 1.6 hectares). Many are subsistence farmers who only grow enough food to support their families. Some Bangladeshi farmers have formed coop-eratives. These growers pool their resources to buy equipment and mar-ket their produce. Altogether, staple and cash crops make up 72 percent of the total value of agricultural goods. The raising of livestock makes up 10 percent, fishing another 10 percent, and forestry 8 percent.

Rice fields dominate the rural landscape of Bangladesh. Rice is grown where farmers can rely on a steady supply of water, either from irriga-tion canals or from rainfall. Farmers raise as many as three crops a year, with the major harvest taking place in November and December.

Bangladeshi men and women work in a **rice field.** Rice is a major agricultural product of Bangladesh.

The jute industry depends on rural growers, who supply the plant that thrives in the country's moist and humid climate. Jute provides a raw material for sacking, though synthetic materials such as nylon are often cheaper. The price of jute has fallen, so many growers have turned to more profitable crops.

Bangladeshi farmers in hilly regions of Chittagong and Sylhet raise tea. This cash crop is second only to jute in total export value. Tobacco farms are common in the north, around the town of Rangpur. Bangladeshi farmers also raise wheat, sugarcane, potatoes, oilseed, and cotton.

Common livestock include cattle, water buffalo, goats, and sheep. Cattle are the major store of wealth for millions of farmers, who raise small herds for their milk, meat, and leather.

Fish is the main source of protein in the nation's diet. Before independence, fishing was the largest industry in the country. It provided a greater share of income than manufacturing. Species of carp, salmon, and catfish inhabit rivers

FISHING WITH OTTERS

With little money available for high-tech equipment, commercial fishing crews in Bangladesh use some low-tech ways to improve their catch. In the Sundarbans and other parts of southern Bangladesh, they work with cast nets in freshwater streams—with the help of trained otters. These small mammals look like weasels. They have webbed feet and can swim for a long time without coming up for air. On command, trained otters dive into the water and chase schools of fish toward the fishing nets.

Men use homemade **fishing nets** in a river near Chittagong. Cast nets are a common way for subsistence farmers to catch fish for their families.

and small ponds, some of them made specifically as fish ponds. On the rivers, fishing crews work from small boats, casting nets or setting traps. Some use trained otters to help gather fish.

Shrimp, crab, lobsters, and other seafood are caught in coastal waters and sent to factories to be processed for export. Assisted by foreign aid and loans, a shrimp farming industry has grown into a major source of export income since the 1980s. Bangladesh is also a major producer of frog legs, with frogs raised on fish farms.

Forests cover about 8 percent of the land in Bangladesh. Most of the forested land is in the hilly regions of the north and east and the Sundarbans of the southwest. With the huge and growing population, however, many forests are fast disappearing. They're being cut down for firewood, construction, or farmland. Several tree species are useful for manufactured products. The wood of gewa trees is processed into soft, pulpy paper, often used as newsprint. Bamboo and teak are used in furniture.

Transportation

In 1998 the road and rail systems of east and west Bangladesh were linked by the Jamuna Bridge. The bridge spans 3 miles (4.8 km) across the Jamuna River.

Bangladesh's network of roads, railways, and water routes struggles to move people from place to place in a crowded region. The Bangladesh Railway started with the British, who linked the Indian region of Assam to the port of Chittagong. The modern railway system covers 1,681 miles (2,706 km) of track. It links 502 stations and all the major cities. Most of the system is built on narrow gauge track. It is not suitable for all trains. New rail construction is adding a third rail to many of these railroads so that any train can use them. Bangladesh has also linked its rail system to India's. A busy direct line runs between Dhaka and Kolkata, India.

The road system expanded in the late twentieth century to a total length of about 13,049 miles (21,000 km). About 10 percent of the system consists of paved, all-weather roads. In a flood-prone country, the paving of roads is a priority, as washed-out roads hinder the movement of people and goods. Throughout Bangladesh, there are about 61,000 cars, 32,000 buses, and 150,000 motorcycles and mopeds in use.

Bangladesh is laced with thousands of rivers, streams, and canals. Water transport is the sole means of travel in many areas. Small canal boats, water taxis, and passenger ferries use the waterways on scheduled service. During the monsoon season, the higher water expands this network to more than 4,971 miles (8,000 km) of navigable water. The Bangladesh Inland Water Transport Authority maintains docks and harbor facilities. Chittagong in the east and Mongla in the west are the major cargo and passenger ports.

Bangladesh has eleven operating airports, with those in Dhaka, Chittagong, and Sylhet handling international traffic. The national carrier, Birman, links eight airports within the country and schedules flights to twenty-six foreign countries.

Communications

The phone system in Bangladesh had a very poor reputation until the first decade of the twenty-first century. The service was unreliable. Customers had to wait months (sometimes years) for the government-run telephone company to install a permanent line. Phone service was limited to urban areas. Rural people had to rely on the mail or telegraph messages to communicate with distant friends or relatives.

The system underwent a big change when the government allowed the establishment of private wireless companies. Aktel, BanglaLink, Grameen Phone, and Teletalk built wireless relay stations and sold inexpensive handsets. With more than nine million cell phones in use, they

A SNAKEY PROFESSION

Charming snakes is an old profession in Bangladesh. Most snake charmers move from town to town. They set up on market days to mesmerize their snakes with the music of flutes and drums. A snake charmers' town has grown up around the village of Porabari, not far from Dhaka. In this settlement of five thousand people, every household includes a snake basket. The profession is slowly dying, however, as environmental problems and the spread of cities has reduced the habitat of cobras and other snakes.

have largely replaced the country's landline services.

Internet service came to Bangladesh in 1996. Since then Internet access has gradually improved in the cities. The growth of the Internet, however, has been slowed by poor infrastructure (such as telephone lines and electricity). Few private homes have personal computers. Investment in Internet service providers (ISPs) has been slow. Fearing political dissent, the government has not taken an active part in building the system. Instead, it closely monitors online activity. The nation has about 450,000 active Internet users, about 0.3 percent of the population.

Mining and Energy

Bangladesh lacks ample mineral and energy resources. Deposits of natural gas, mostly in the northeast, have been exploited as an energy source and to produce fertilizer. Gas has also been found in the Bay of Bengal, where companies explore for oil deposits. Underwater drilling is expensive, however, and the country needs foreign investment to extract these resources. The Karnaphuli Dam, meanwhile, provides renewable energy to some parts of the country.

Coal reserves in northern Bangladesh lie more than 3,000 feet (914 m) beneath the surface. They are expensive to mine. Silica sand is used in cement production. Marine salt is produced along the coast. Deposits of kaolin provide the raw material for pottery. Bangladesh also has deposits of limestone in the districts of Sylhet and Chittagong.

EPZs

Bangladesh has established eight export processing zones (EPZs) to stimulate its economy. The EPZs allow foreign companies to operate without the burden of licensing fees and income taxes faced by domestic industries. The EPZs invite foreign companies to relocate from other low-wage countries. The zones benefit these companies by providing useful infrastructure, such as exclusive telephone exchanges and self-contained power plants, but wages for workers are low.

Foreign Trade

With limited manufacturing and natural resources and with most of its people working as subsistence farmers, Bangladesh carries out much less foreign trade than its neighbors India and Myanmar. Its main exports—shirts, blouses, pants, and other ready-made clothing—are manufactured in hundreds of small textile factories, most established in Dhaka and other cities by foreign companies. Bangladesh also sells leather goods—mostly shoes—and jute, although the market in jute has been shrinking for decades.

The most important agricultural exports, shrimp and fish, have been growing steadily, as new fish farms produce a reliable supply.

Bangladesh imports raw textiles, machinery, steel, chemicals, crude oil, vegetable oil, transportation equipment, and plastics. The country imports much more than it exports, creating a trade deficit of about $4 billion per year. This deficit is largely made up by money sent home from Bangladeshi workers living abroad. Foreign aid also helps. Aid arrives from European countries, Japan, and donor organizations such as the United Nations Children's Fund (UNICEF) and the Asian Development Bank. The nation's most important commercial trading partners are India, China, Singapore, South Korea, Japan, and the United States.

WORKING ABROAD

Many Bangladeshi men leave home in search of jobs—mainly construction—in the Middle East. Bangladeshis make up a large part of the workforce in Qatar, Dubai, Saudi Arabia, Oman, and Kuwait. They earn low wages—usually just several hundred dollars a month—and live in large workers' barracks. Their jobs are often dangerous, but many stay on their worksites for years. They send home nearly $5 billion to their families every year.

The Future

Bangladesh has had a turbulent history since its founding in 1971. The country has experienced social turmoil and violence, economic troubles, and natural disasters. The rivalry between the two major political parties has destabilized the country, encouraging rural people to move to the cities and productive workers to migrate abroad. In addition, foreign countries avoid making the investment needed by Bangladesh's energy projects and manufacturing industries.

The country does have some advantages as it heads into the future. The huge pool of laborers in Bangladesh attracts foreign companies, which benefit from the country's low costs and wages. This foreign investment may expand to include high-tech industries. To encourage outside investment, the government of Bangladesh has lowered export fees and taxes to outside companies and privatized (removed government control of) many industries. If Bangladesh can establish a thriving technology industry, the country's people may benefit from a rising standard of living.

The key to this future is the political system, which has failed the country through dictatorship, violence, and corruption. If the leaders of Bangladesh can put aside their historic differences and cooperate in the making of laws and policy, the country has a chance at a peaceful and more prosperous future.

1000 B.C. The Bang people settle in the lower Ganges River valley, giving their name to Bengal and later the nation of Bangladesh.

330s B.C. The strength of the Gangaridai Empire discourages conquest by the Macedonians under Alexander the Great.

322 B.C. King Chandragupta Maurya founds the Mauryan Empire.

273 B.C. King Asoka begins his reign, a time in which Buddhism arrives in Bengal.

A.D. 200s The Gupta dynasty increases its power across northern India and reaches the lower Ganges River valley and Bengal.

550 The Gupta dynasty collapses.

750 Gopala founds the Buddhist Pala dynasty. Under the Pala kings, Bengal exports its religion and artistic styles to Southeast Asia, Tibet, and Indonesia.

1095 Prince Hemanta Sen overthrows the Pala king and the Sena dynasty.

1205 A Muslim army invades Bengal and brings the region under the control of sultans who rule from the city of Delhi, India.

1342 An ambitious Persian noble, Ilias Shah, establishes a new dynasty in Bengal and plans a campaign of conquest in eastern India and the Himalayas.

1414 King Ganesha returns Bengal to the traditional beliefs of Hinduism.

1435 King Nasiruddin Mahmud suppresses Hindu beliefs and promotes Islam.

1534 Sher Shah Suri, an Afghan commander of the Delhi sultanate, invades Bengal and proclaims independence from the sultan.

1576 The Mughal Empire conquers Bengal and incorporates the region into its domain.

1608 The capital of the Mughal province of Bengal moves to the city of Dhaka.

1658 The sultan Aurangzeb comes to power. He opposes the growing presence of British merchants and colonists in Bengal.

1757 The East India Company wrests control of Bengal from the weakening Mughal Empire.

1764 The British defeat the forces of the nawab of Bengal and the Mughal sultan at the Battle of Buxar.

1834 The East Indian Company becomes an arm of the British government.

1857 The Sepoy Rebellion erupts among Indians opposed to British rule.

1885 Bengali Hindus opposed to British control of their administration and trade join the Indian National Congress.

1905 Great Britain divides the region into East Bengal and West Bengal.

1906 Muslims establish the All-India Muslim League to fight for rights and
independence of Muslims in India.

1912 In the face of widespread opposition, Great Britain ends the division of Bengal.

1913 Rabindranath Tagore wins the Nobel Prize in Literature.

1939 World War II breaks out in Europe, where Great Britain declares war on Germany.
The British administration of India declares its support for the war effort
against Germany.

1940 Muslim leaders adopt the Lahore Resolution, calling for a separate state for
Muslim-majority areas of northwestern India and Bengal.

1947 India wins independence from British rule. In areas with a Muslim majority, the nation
of Pakistan is established, divided into Pakistan and East Bengal, which is later named
East Pakistan.

1952 The Bengali Language Movement leads to clashes with demonstrators, who favor the
autonomy of East Bengal.

1958 General Mohammad Ayub Khan seizes power in Pakistan.

1965 General Khan wins Pakistan's first presidential elections.

1970 A monsoon devastates East Pakistan, killing more than one million people and flooding
over half the arable (agricultural) land.

1971 India helps East Pakistan achieve independence in the Indo-Pakistani War of 1971. East
Pakistan breaks away and becomes independent Bangladesh.

1972 The parliament of Bangladesh passes a constitution.

1976 General Ziaur Rahman imposes a military dictatorship and martial law.

1991 Khaleda Zia becomes the prime minister after General Ershad is forced out of office.

2001 Zia is elected prime minister for the second time.

2006 Strikes disrupt the textile industry, and violence spreads as workers demand
better wages and working conditions. Muhammad Yunus wins the Nobel Peace
Prize for his microcredit business through Grameen Bank.

2007 A caretaker government controls Bangladesh after elections are suspended
and the prime minister resigns.

2008 A European Union committee on climate change announces that Bangladesh,
with so much of its land barely above sea level, could be one of the countries hardest hit by global warming and rising ocean levels.

COUNTRY NAME People's Republic of Bangladesh

AREA 55,598 square miles (144,000 sq. km)

MAIN LANDFORMS Bangladesh Plain, Chittagong Hills, Mouths of the Ganges, Sylhet Hills

HIGHEST POINTS unnamed peak, 3,451 feet (1,052 m); Mount Keokradong, 3,196 feet (974 m)

MAJOR RIVERS Ganges, Jamuna, Karnaphuli, Meghna, Padma

ANIMALS bears, Bengal tigers, cranes, crocodiles, deer, ducks, frogs, geese, gibbons, lizards, rhinoceroses, snakes, turtles, water buffalo

CAPITAL CITY Dhaka

OTHER MAJOR CITIES Chittagong, Khulna, Rajshahi

OFFICIAL LANGUAGE Bengali (Bangla)

MONETARY UNIT Taka. 1 taka = 100 paisa

BANGLADESHI CURRENCY

The money of Bangladesh, the taka, comes in coins of 1 and 5 taka and paper notes of 1, 2, 5, 10, 20, 50, 100, and 500 taka. Paisa coins are available in denominations of 1, 5, 10, 25, and 50.

The exchange rate between the taka and the U.S. dollar varies. But in the first decade of the twenty-first century, it stood at about 50 taka to $1.

Taka notes carry images evoking the history, religion, industry, and independence of Bangladesh. Sheikh Mujibur Rahman, the leader of the Bangladesh independence movement, appears on the 100- and 500-taka notes. The paper money also shows industries, a hydroelectric dam, a modern bridge, rice cultivation, and the spotted deer. The 2-taka note shows the doel, the national bird, and an image of the Language Martyrs' Monument, a famous landmark in Dhaka that commemorates the fight for Bengali language and culture during the 1950s.

Bangladesh adopted its flag in 1972. The flag was adapted from a banner designed by Bangladeshi artist Quamrul Hassan during the fight for freedom in 1971. The red disc symbolizes the sun and the blood being shed. The modified flag shows a simple design of a red disc on a green rectangle. The green symbolizes the country's well-watered and fertile fields.

Rabindranath Tagore wrote "Amar Shonar Bangla," (My Golden Bengal), the national anthem of Bangladesh. Tagore wrote the poem in 1906. Great Britain had just divided Bengal in half. The split raised a strong spirit of Bengali nationalism and independence. In 1972 the government of Bangladesh adopted "Amar Shonar Bangla" as the nation's national anthem.

"Amar Shonar Bangla"

My Bengal of gold,
I love you.
Forever your skies,
Your air set my heart in tune
As if it were a flute,
In spring, Oh mother mine,
The fragrance from your mango groves
Makes me wild with joy,
Ah, what a thrill!
In autumn, Oh mother mine,
In the full-blossomed paddy fields,
I have seen spread all over sweet smiles!

Ah, what a beauty, what shades,
What an affection and what a tenderness!
What a quilt have you spread
At the feet of banyan trees
And along the banks of rivers!
Oh mother mine, words from your lips
Are like nectar to my ears!
Ah, what a thrill!
If sadness, Oh mother mine,
Casts a gloom on your face,
My eyes are filled with tears!

Visit www.vgsbooks.com for links to hear Bangladesh's national anthem, "Amar Shonar Bangla."

Flag National Anthem

TARAMON BIBI (b. 1956) Born in the village of Shankar Madhapur, Taramon Bibi was a veteran of the 1971 war for independence. She joined a guerrilla group as a young farm girl, shortly before the war began. She fought courageously and was awarded a medal for valor by the government. She didn't know that she'd earned the honor, however, and her location was unknown for years until a researcher found her in 1995. The prime minister presented Bibi with her medal during a ceremony in Dhaka.

BROJEN DAS (1927–1998) Das was born in the village of Kuchiamora and attended college in Kolkata. He was a champion freestyle swimmer through the 1950s and competed for Pakistan in the 1956 Summer Olympics in Melbourne, Australia. In 1958 he took part in several long-distance swimming exhibitions, including a swim in Italy from the island of Capri to Naples—a distance of 21 miles (33 km). In the same year, he won a race across the English Channel, becoming the first Asian to accomplish the swim from Great Britain to France. In 1961 he set a world record time of 10 hours 35 minutes for a swim across the English Channel.

KHWAJA ABDUL GHANI (1813–1896) A nawab of Dhaka who played an important role in the history of East Bengal, Ghani was born in Dhaka into a landowning family. He built a new system of roads, a public water supply, and streetlights in Dhaka. He also set aside land for parks and the national zoo. He published the first English newspaper in Dhaka, the *Weekly Dhaka News*. He strived to lessen tension among the different religious communities of the city.

RANI HAMID (b. 1944) A chess player born in Sylhet, Rani Hamid won the title of Women's International Master in 1985. She is the only Bangladeshi chess player to gain this honor. She has won several championships in Great Britain and has been the undisputed women's champion in Bangladesh for more than thirty years. Her international matches are followed closely at home by Bangladeshis, who have made her a national hero.

KAZEM ALI QURESHI (1857–1951) A poet born in Agla, near Dhaka, Qureshi is known by his pen name, Kaykobad. He is revered as one of the foremost poets in the Bengali language. He worked as a postmaster in his native village while creating long works such as *The Great Crematorium*, a poem dealing with the horrors of war. He also wrote about Muslim religious tradition and the long conflict between Hindus and Muslims in Bengal.

SHEIKH MUJIBUR RAHMAN (1920–1975) This political leader, better known as Sheikh Mujib, was born in Tungipara. He founded the Awami League, which fought for the independence of Bangladesh. His arrest by the Pakistan government helped touch off the conflict of 1971, which led to the end of West Pakistan's rule of East Pakistan. He served as first president of Bangladesh and later as prime minister. His rule inspired intense opposition, however. He was assassinated in 1975 by members of the army.

RABINDRANATH TAGORE (1861–1941) A world-renowned Bengali poet, novelist, artist, and composer, Tagore was born in Kolkata, India, and spent much of his life in the town of Shilaidaha. He began writing at an early age. He won the Nobel Prize in Literature in 1913 and a knighthood from the British Crown in 1915. He was a strong supporter of Indian independence. He remains a cultural icon in Bangladesh, where his songs make up an entire musical genre of their own.

PRITILATA WADDEDAR (1911–1932) A pro-independence militant when East Bengal was under the control of the British, Waddedar was born in Chittagong. She joined the pro-independence underground movement and led an attack on a private British club on the night of September 23, 1932. She was captured and committed suicide, becoming a martyr to the cause of independence.

MUHAMMAD YUNUS (b. 1940) The founder of Grameen Bank, Yunus is a pioneer of the microcredit business that extends small business loans to the poor. Born in the village of Bathua near Chittagong, he worked as an economics professor in Bangladesh and the United States. He made his first loans in 1976 to a group of village women building bamboo furniture. The business developed into the Grameen Bank in 1983. In 2006 Yunus was awarded the Nobel Peace Prize.

KHALEDA ZIA (b. 1945) Born in Dinajpur, Zia is the leader of the Bangladesh Nationalist Party. She was the first female prime minister of Bangladesh, serving terms from 1991 to 1996 and from 2001 to 2006. In her first term, her government introduced compulsory and free education for students in primary school. Violence and charges of corruption and vote-rigging plagued her second term in office.

COX'S BAZAAR This town on the Bay of Bengal lies in southeastern Bangladesh, near the border with Myanmar. The beach—the longest in the world—measures 75 miles (121 km). It is one of the best surfing beaches in south Asia. In places the beach is lined with temples and shrines.

DHAKESHWARI TEMPLE The country's most famous Hindu shrine stands in Dhaka. It contains four large statues of the god Shiva. Each year the temple hosts the fervent puja (worship) of the warrior goddess Durga.

KANTAJEES TEMPLE This elaborate Hindu temple near the town of Dinajpur was built in the eighteenth century. The entire temple is covered with beautifully designed plaques and wall paintings. They show mythological scenes, wildlife, geometric designs, and scenes of daily life.

LANGUAGE MARTYRS' MONUMENT This monument in Dhaka commemorates the deaths of students at the hands of the police on February 21, 1952. The students were protesting the imposition of the Urdu language on East Pakistan by the government of Pakistan. The monument is the site of solemn celebrations every February 21, Martyrs' Day.

LAWACHARA FOREST This rain forest preserve in the Sylhet region has abundant wildlife, including gibbons, colorful parrots, pythons, and deer. Visitors can explore this vibrant forest and see its 160 plant, 246 bird, and 30 animal species.

MAHASTHANGARH The oldest archaeological site in Bangladesh, this ancient city was the capital of several important dynasties from the third millennium B.C. The city was contained in a square area surrounded by walls 15 feet (4.5 m) high and about a mile (1.6 km) long on each side. The ancient walls still rise over the surrounding rice fields.

PAHARPUR This is a solemn and peaceful Buddhist monastery built in northern Bangladesh in the seventh century. It is the largest Buddhist monastery south of the Himalayas.

SRIMANGAL In the eighteenth century, as the British took control of Bengal, this area became an important center of tea growing. The area has more than one hundred tea gardens and plantations, as well as a tea research center open to visitors.

STAR MOSQUE This famous Muslim shrine in Dhaka has five domes covered in bright white porcelain, to give the impression of twinkling stars. The interior of the mosque has elaborate mosaic floors, walls, and ceilings.

SYLHET VALLEY This area surrounds the confluence of the Surma and Kushiara rivers. Millions of migrating birds fly here each winter from Siberia and across the Himalayas.

Awami League: a group founded in the 1950s that fought for the dominance of the Bengali language in East Pakistan and then for the complete independence of Bangladesh. The Awami League is one of the two major political parties in the country.

Chaltibhasa: one of the two principal forms of Bengali as it is spoken in Bangladesh. Chaltibhasa is used for everyday conversation

coup: the sudden, often violent, overthrow of a government

gross domestic product (GDP): the value of the goods and services produced by a country over a period of time, usually one year

guerrilla: independent group or individuals carrying out unofficial warfare, including sabotage

jatra: open-air theaters that entertain Bangladeshi villagers with familiar characters and plots

Jumma: a name for the hill tribes of the Chittagong region, whose traditional culture is closely related to that of western Myanmar

jute: a tall, slender plant that grows in Bangladesh's well-watered soil and whose fibers go into twine, sacking, and textiles

kabaddi: a popular team sport that pits two squads of players on a marked court. Players hold their breath as they run to the opposing side's territory to tag or hold opponents.

kaolin: a white clay used in the production of pottery, still an important industry in Bangladesh

Pahela Baishakh: This phrase for the Bangladesh New Year celebration means "early morning start." It takes place in spring every year and is celebrated with special foods and street parties.

Rabindra Sangeet: the body of more than two thousand poems composed by Rabindranath Tagore. They make up an important musical form in modern Bangladesh.

Sadhubhasa: a complex and formal version of Bengali, used for literary works and official documents

sepoys: Indian soldiers employed in the British army. The sepoys held a subordinate (lesser) status to British officers, a role that caused resentment and led to a full-scale mutiny known as the Sepoy Rebellion during the 1850s.

tiffin: the traditional late-afternoon teatime introduced to Bangladesh by the British during colonial times and that still takes place in Bangladesh

zamindars: administrators and tax collectors during the time of the Mughal Empire. The zamindar system was adopted by the British and used until the twentieth century.

zila: one of the sixty-four districts into which Bangladesh is divided

Selected Bibliography

Barker, Amanda. *Bangladesh*. Portsmouth, NH: Heinemann, 1994.
This comprehensive portrait of Bangladesh includes its politics, culture, geography, and religion. Case studies of individuals paint the picture of the nation's varied community.

Baxter, Craig. *Bangladesh: From a Nation to a State*. Boulder, CO: Westview Press, 1997.
The author describes the modern political history of Bangladesh, from its time as a part of British India to the era of independence.

CIA. *The World Factbook: Bangladesh*. 2007.
https://www.cia.gov/library/publications/the-world-factbook/geos/bg.html (January 30, 2008).
This source offers statistics and background information on Bangladesh's economy, history, demographics, and more.

Glassie, Henry. *Art and Life in Bangladesh*. Bloomington: Indiana University Press, 1997.
The author explores the handmade crafts of Bangladesh, including pottery, rug weaving, boatbuilding, sculpture, engraving, and painting, giving historical context to the distinctive styles that have developed among modern village artists.

Hashmi, Taj ul-Islam. *Women and Islam in Bangladesh: Beyond Subjection and Tyranny*. London: Palgrave Macmillan, 2000.
This book describes the position of women in the history of Bangladesh and how women live, work, and act within a modern Muslim society. The author believes that better education and literacy and an improvement in the national economy would substantially improve the lives of women and end their subservient position.

Heitzman, James. *Bangladesh: A Country Study*. Washington, DC: US Government Printing Office, 1989.
This guide includes a detailed history of the country as well as insight into its politics and economy. An online update is available at http://lcweb2.loc.gov/frd/cs/bdtoc.html.

Jahan, Rounaq, ed. *Bangladesh: Promise and Performance*. London: Zed Books, 2001.
In this series of essays, several scholars tackle pressing political, economic, and social issues of modern Bangladesh.

Karlekar, Hiranmay. *Bangladesh: The Next Afghanistan?* London: Sage Publications, 2005.
The author believes that terrorists are trying to undermine Bangladesh's political system and destroy the country's tolerant attitude toward various religious faiths and sects.

McAdam, Marika. *Lonely Planet: Bangladesh*. Footscray, Victoria, AUS: Lonely Planet Publications, 2004.
This is a tourist's guide to Bangladesh, with listings of attractions, hotels, restaurants, and sights to see.

Mintoo, Abdul Awal. *Bangladesh: Anatomy of Change.* **Twickenham, UK: Athena Press Publishing, 2006.**
Political corruption and economic mismanagement in Bangladesh has brought about the country's dire poverty, according to this author. The author suggests how Bangladesh can join the new global economy.

Monan, Jim. *Bangladesh: The Strength to Succeed.* **London: Oxfam, 1995.**
This book examines the many problems and challenges faced by the people of Bangladesh, emphasizing the effects of British colonialism and an economic system that benefits a small elite group of wealthy landowners and industrialists.

PRB. "PRB 2006 World Population Data Sheet." *Population Reference Bureau (PRB).* **2006.**
http://www.prb.org (December 26, 2007).
This annual statistics sheet provides a wealth of data on Bangladesh's population, birthrates and death rates, fertility rate, infant mortality rate, and other useful demographic information.

Riaz, Ali. *God Willing: The Politics of Islamism in Bangladesh.* **Lanham, MD: Rowman & Littlefield, 2004.**
The author examines the growing strength of militant Islamic groups within Bangladesh and the possibility of these groups exploiting the country's political turmoil to establish a fundamentalist Islamic state.

U.S. Department of State: Bureau of European and Eurasian Affairs. "Bangladesh." *Background Notes.* **2007.**
http://www.state.gov/r/pa/ei/bgn/3452.htm (January 30, 2008).
This overview, published annually and regularly updated by the U.S. government, provides an introduction to Bangladesh's government, history, foreign relations, and more.

Yunus, Muhammad. *Banker to the Poor: Micro-Lending and the Battle against World Poverty.* **New York: Public Affairs, 2003.**
The founder of microcredit banking describes how he began by extending small loans to the poor, so they could start and run small businesses. The idea succeeded, and more than fifty countries operate similar microcredit industries.

———. *Creating a World without Poverty: Social Business and the Future of Capitalism.* New York: Public Affairs, 2007.
Yunus describes a business model that combines the free market system with a responsibility to operate in a more humane world. He explains his theory that capitalism can be used as a tool to raise up, rather than exploit, the poor.

AsiaRecipe.com
http://www.asiarecipe.com/bangladesh.html
This site offers many recipes for Bangladeshi meals as well as a background on culture, religion, art, and more.

Baldizzone, Tiziana, and Gianni Baldizzone. *Tales from the River Brahmaputra*. Boston: Shambhala, 1998.
This book features stories and hundreds of photographs of the meandering Brahmaputra River, from its sources in the Himalayas to its mouth on the Bay of Bengal.

Bangladesh ShowBiz
http://www.bangladeshshowbiz.com/
This site covers movies, music, and culture, with MP3 downloads, gossip, movie reviews, radio and television features, and current entertainment events from Bangladesh.

Banglapedia.com
http://banglapedia.org/
This website presents the ten-volume national encyclopedia of Bangladesh, with thousands of entries in English and Bengali on the history, politics, arts, and culture of the country. The entries are hyperlinked, making it easy to explore and understand unfamiliar words and topics.

BBC News, Country Profile: Bangladesh
http://news.bbc.co.uk/1/hi/world/south_asia/country_profiles/1160598.stm
The BBC's country profile of Bangladesh gives an overview of the nation, some fast facts, information about current leaders, and news updates.

Buerk, Roland. *Breaking Ships: How Supertankers and Cargo Ships Are Dismantled on the Beaches of Bangladesh*. New York: Chamberlain Brothers, 2006.
The author describes the complex and dangerous business of dismantling huge oceangoing ships, a major industry in the city of Chittagong.

Eaton, Richard M. *The Rise of Islam and the Bengal Frontier*. Berkeley: University of California Press, 1996.
The author explores the emergence of Islam in Bengal and how the new faith shaped the culture and government of that region under the Mughal emperors.

Engfer, Lee. *India in Pictures*. Minneapolis: Twenty-First Century Books, 2003.
Learn more about the geography, history, people, culture, and economy of Bangladesh's neighbor.

Frater, Alexander. *Chasing the Monsoon*. New York: Picador, 2005.
The author traveled through the Indian subcontinent, exploring the effects of the rainy season on the people of Bangladesh and India.

Further Reading and Websites

Government of the People's Republic of Bangladesh
http://www.bangladeshgov.org
The official website of the national government provides information on the various government ministries, a full text of the constitution, maps of the country, and links to various Bengali and English newspapers.

Hartmann, Betsy, and James K. Boyce. *Quiet Violence: View from a Bangladesh Village.* Oakland: Food First, 1985.
The authors lived in a poor village in Bangladesh for nine months to write this book about the struggle of neighboring families to survive.

Nasrin, Taslima. *Meyebela: My Bengali Girlhood.* Hanover, NH: Steerforth, 1998.
In this memoir, a renowned Bangladeshi author describes her strict, sometimes cruel upbringing in a Muslim family. After reaching adulthood, the author fled the country after receiving threats on her life for her criticism of the treatment of women in Bangladesh. This book was banned in Bangladesh soon after it was published.

Taus-Bolstad, Stacy. *Pakistan in Pictures.* Minneapolis: Twenty-First Century Books, 2003.
Learn about the history between Bangladesh and Pakistan, as well as information about the geography, people, culture, and economy of Pakistan.

Travel Bangladesh
http://www.bangladesh.com
This visitor's guide to Bangladesh lists flights to the country, hotels, tourist attractions, religious festivals, and holidays.

vgsbooks.com
http://www.vgsbooks.com
Visit vgsbooks.com, the home page of the Visual Geography Series®. You can get linked to all sorts of useful online information, including geographical, historical, demographic, cultural, and economic websites. The vgsbooks.com site is a great resource for late-breaking news and statistics.

Virtual Bangladesh
http://www.virtualbangladesh.com
Visitors will learn about Bangladesh, its history, culture, and language on this site. Images, sounds, and text describe Bangladesh and its people.

Whyte, Mariam. *Bangladesh.* Tarrytown, NY: Marshall Cavendish, 1999.
This introduction to Bangladesh is part of the Cultures of the World series. It includes a detailed description of the history and physical appearance of the country, as well as a guide to its culture.

Captions for photos appearing on cover and chapter openers:

Cover: Fishing crews set up shrimp nets from their boats on a river in Bangladesh. Shrimp and other seafood are important exports for Bangladesh.

pp. 4–5 Rickshaws crowd a busy street in Bangladesh's capital city, Dhaka.

pp. 8–9 The city of Sylhet is on the banks of the Surma River in northeastern Bangladesh.

pp. 20–21 The parliament building in Dhaka is where the lawmakers of the Jatiyo Sangshad (Bangladesh's parliament) meet.

pp. 38–39 These children live in a village in northern Bangladesh.

pp. 46–47 Star Mosque in Dhaka is more than two hundred years old. The mosque has five domes and gets its name from the hundreds of stars on its surface.

pp. 56–57 Women drench jute in a river to extract the jute fibers. Jute is used to make twine and sacks for some agricultural goods.

Photo Acknowledgments
The images in this book are used with the permission of: © Dave Saunders/ Art Directors, pp. 4-5, 8-9, 14, 18, 19, 20-21, 51, 54; © XNR Productions, pp. 6, 10; © Abdul Malek Babul/Drik/Majority World/The Image Works, p. 11; © Nicholas Pitt/Alamy, p. 12; © Larry Burrows/Time & Life Pictures/Getty Images, p. 13; AP Photo/Pavel Rahman, pp. 15, 52 (right); © Images&Stories/ Alamy, p. 17; © Mustafiz Mamun/Drik/Majority World/The Image Works, p. 24; Rue des Archives/The Granger Collection, New York, p. 27; Library of Congress (LC-D426-580), p. 29; © Amanda Schutz, pp. 31, 45; © Abdul Hamid Raihan/Drik/Majority World/The Image Works, p. 32; © John Garrett/ Art Directors, p. 33; © Reuters/CORBIS, p. 35 (top); © Bal Krishnan/Drik/ Majority World/The Image Works, p. 35 (bottom); AP Photo/Press Information Department of Government of Bangladesh, HO, p. 37; © Borderlands/Alamy, pp. 38-39; © Cory Langley, pp. 40, 42, 60, 62; AP Photo/Gary Knight, p. 44; © Trip/Art Directors, pp. 46-47, 61; AP Photo, p. 49 (both); © Farjana K. Godhuly/AFP/Getty Images, p. 52 (left); © Karen Robinson/Panos Pictures, pp. 56-57; © Jenny Matthews/Alamy, p. 59; Audrius Tomonis–www.banknotes. com, p. 68, © Laura Westlund/Independent Picture Service, p. 69.

Front Cover: © Images&Stories/Alamy. Back Cover: NASA.